KIRSTIN BLAISE LOBATO'S
UNREASONABLE CONVICTION

Possibility Of Guilt Replaces Proof Beyond A Reasonable Doubt

By Hans Sherrer

Published February 2008 by:

The Justice Institute
PO Box 68911
Seattle, WA 98168

http://justicedenied.org
info@justicedenied.org

ISBN: 1434843254
EAN-13: 9781434843258

Third printing

Table of Contents

Highlight Boxes

Maps

Photos

Preface

Wrongful convictions of factually innocent people are an inescapable feature of the legal system in the United States. I can attest to that as publisher of *Justice:Denied – the magazine for the wrongly convicted*. Although a wrongful conviction can involve a wide variety of circumstances, I am particularly intrigued by a case that involves a person with evidence of having been in another city, state, or even country, at the time the crime was committed of which he or she was convicted.

Consequently, my interest was piqued by a case involving an 18-year-old woman convicted in May 2002 of murdering a homeless man and sexually assaulting his corpse in Las Vegas on July 8, 2001. Why? The young woman has the alibi that the entire day of the murder she was 170 miles north of Las Vegas at her parent's house in Panaca, Nevada. That young woman is Kirstin Blaise Lobato, who is known by her middle name of Blaise.

More than a year after becoming aware of Blaise's case, an article I wrote about her case was published in *Justice:Denied's* Fall 2004 issue. About the same time the Nevada Supreme Court reversed her convictions on September 3, 2004, and ordered her retrial. The decision was based on evidentiary rulings by the trial judge that prejudiced Blaise's right to a fair trial.

After a near carbon copy retrial by the prosecution, in October 2006 Blaise was again convicted of sexually assaulting Bailey's corpse, but of voluntary manslaughter instead of first-degree murder as she had been after her first trial. I responded by writing a second article about her case that was published in *Justice:Denied's* Fall 2006 issue.

Although the two *Justice:Denied* articles were informative, important facets of Blaise's case can only be fleshed out in the longer form of a book. Among other things it enables the presentation of tables and graphs that aid visualizing such things as the details of Blaise's alibi, and that there is a lack of intersection between the details in her police statement and the peculiar facts of the man's murder. You may want to keep in mind while reading this that many of the hundreds of endnotes marked throughout the text have additional details.

Any recital of a protracted legal case involving two trials must necessarily focus on the details that allow the reader to generally understand what happened and the basic issues. Consequently, considerable editorial judgment has been exercised in separating the wheat from the chaff in the course of writing this almost 60,000 word account.

The Nevada Supreme Court is currently considering Blaise's appeal of her October 2006 convictions, so we know there is at least one chapter to her story that has yet to be written.

Hans Sherrer
February 2008

Introduction

Kirstin Blaise Lobato, who goes by her middle name, has twice been convicted of charges relating to the savage murder and treatment of the body of a homeless man, Duran Bailey, in Las Vegas on July 8, 2001. She was convicted in May 2002 of first-degree murder and sexual penetration of a dead body, and sentenced to a minimum of 40 years in prison. After a retrial ordered by the Nevada Supreme Court, she was again convicted in October 2006, but of voluntary manslaughter and sexual penetration of a dead body, and sentenced to a minimum of 13 years in prison.

What is odd about those convictions is there is neither any physical or forensic evidence, nor any eyewitness or confession linking the then one-hundred pound 18-year-old Blaise to Bailey's physically brutal murder and sexual mutilation that is described by experts as having homosexual overtones. Nor is there a single witness or any other evidence that places her or her car in Las Vegas on the day of Bailey's death (or for nearly a week preceding it). In contrast, more than a dozen witnesses have sworn under oath that they saw Blaise from July 2 to July 9 while she was staying at her parent's house in Panaca, a small Lincoln County town 170 miles north of Las Vegas. Blaise's presence in and around Panaca is corroborated by medical records, and telephone records of her numerous and daily conversations with a male friend in Las Vegas. Consistent with her continuous presence in Panaca is that multiple witnesses have sworn that they did not see her car moved after she parked it in front of her parent's house on July 2 until it was taken away by a tow truck on July 20, 2001.

The prosecution's contention that Blaise murdered Bailey is also undermined by the tested crime scene evidence. That evidence includes fingerprints that exclude her, bloody shoeprints leading away from Bailey's body that exclude her, the DNA test of chewing gum found on the cardboard covering Bailey's body that excludes her, the DNA test of two cigarette butts found on Bailey's body that excludes her, the DNA test of a pubic hair found on Bailey's body that is excluded as being either his or hers, the confirmatory test of several possibly faint iron spots inside her 17-year-old used car (1984 Fiero) that are excluded as blood, and her car is excluded as the source of tire tracks near Bailey's body. In addition, no evidence was found in Blaise's possession or in her car that directly or through forensic testing links her to Bailey's murder or the crime scene. Neither did Blaise have any injuries, or even bruises or cuts on her hands that would be expected to be visible on the person who inflicted the vigorous beating and stabbing of Bailey – particularly a person of Blaise's slight physique.

Furthermore, at the time of Blaise's trials, and to this day, there is no evidence that she had ever met Bailey, that she knew anyone acquainted with Bailey, or that she had ever been to the west Las Vegas bank parking lot where Bailey's body was found in the trash enclosure where he lived.

So what was the evidence relied on by the prosecution to link Blaise to Bailey's murder? Las Vegas Metropolitan Police Department homicide detective Thomas Thowsen decided to arrest Blaise and charge her with Bailey's murder on the basis of third-hand gossip provided to him over the telephone on July 20, 2001 by Laura Johnson, Lincoln County's juvenile probation officer. Johnson told Thowsen that a former teacher of Blaises' said that Blaise told the teacher about using a knife to fend off a Las Vegas sexual assault during which the man's penis may have been severed. The teacher was Dixie Tienken. Thowsen, however, made no attempt to contact Tienken by telephone, email or through her work as a Lincoln County teacher to verify Johnson's account. Instead, he made the snap decision that Blaise was guilty of Bailey's murder.

Thowsen, his partner James LaRochelle, and a crime scene analyst drove up to Lincoln County on the afternoon of Johnson's phone call to arrest Blaise and seize her car for transport back to Las Vegas for examination by the police crime lab. After Johnson made a taped statement, the detectives arranged for a tow truck to transport Blaise's car to Las Vegas, and they enlisted local sheriff deputies to accompany them to the nearby home of Blaise's parents to arrest her. The detectives made no attempt to contact Tienken to confirm Johnson's account – even though she lived in Panaca only blocks from the home of Blaise's parents.

Upon arriving the detectives didn't tell Blaise she was under arrest for Bailey's murder – which she *de facto* was. If she had tried to leave they would have shot her in the back if they thought it was necessary to stop her. After all, they believed she was a murderer. Although the detectives were likely hoping she would confess, Blaise didn't say anything during a 26-minute audio recorded statement incriminating her in Bailey's murder or that even suggested she had been in Las Vegas on the day he was murdered. The detectives knew the details of Bailey's murder, and the many details Blaise provided in her statement of the assault against her clearly identified it as a different incident. (16 of those differences are in Table 1, p. 17) Among those details is her attacker was alive when she got away after she cut at his penis one time in the dark; it occurred weeks prior to Bailey's murder; and it happened in a different part of Las Vegas many miles from the scene of Bailey's murder. However, the lack of an incriminating statement by Blaise was irrelevant to the detectives because they made the nearly three hour drive to Panaca to arrest her, not to conduct an investigation and gather credible evidence either corroborating or disproving Johnson's third-hand gossip.

Although it was more apparent in Blaise's second trial, Johnson was the prosecution's indispensable "star witness" because of her status as a law enforcement officer, and she was adamant about what she claimed Tienken told her Blaise said. Tienken on the other hand, has insisted that when Thowsen interviewed her six days after Blaise's arrest, he attempted to influence her to mold her recollections of her conversation with Johnson to what he wanted her to say – and in a way that would have supported Johnson's statement. [1] Johnson's indispensable role in Blaise's convictions was commensurate with the fact that Blaise was arrested for Bailey's murder on the basis of the third-hand gossip Johnson told Thowsen during their initial telephone conversation.

On the surface it might seem ridiculous that a teenage girl with a slight build could be accused of causing the multitude of extensive physical injuries inflicted on Bailey, particularly without sustaining any injuries herself or even a bruise. It might also seem ridiculous, as the prosecution contended at Blaise's trials, that she specifically drove the 340 mile round-trip from Panaca to Las Vegas to buy methamphetamines from the homeless Bailey when it was readily available minutes from her parent's house in Lincoln County. That contention is also absurd because Bailey *didn't use* meth, *didn't have* any meth, *didn't sell* meth to anyone and there is no evidence Blaise knew him. As much as those things stretch credulity, it is even more ridiculous that Blaise could be seriously accused of murdering Bailey in Las Vegas when there is considerable unrebutted alibi evidence that she was 170 miles away in Panaca the entire day of his murder on July 8, 2001.

The substantial forensic, physical, documentary, medical, alibi and circumstantial evidence in Blaise's case that excludes her from any involvement in Bailey's murder, and the absence of evidence linking her to his murder, is why the prosecution's case against Blaise is based on the argument that the possibility she might have killed him can't be 100% ruled out, and therefore she must be guilty.

But as British statesman and naturalist Sir John Lubbock observed more than a century ago, "What we see depends mainly on what we look for." The people looking for Blaise's guilt have only seen that because that is what they were looking for. Looking for the truth of Bailey's murder reveals a much different picture – and Blaise is nowhere to be found in that picture.

This account of Blaise's case is based on sources that include the pretrial and trial record of Blaise's two trials, interviews with some of the witnesses, and extra-judicial statements by witnesses. We are told over and over that in this country a person is presumed innocent of a crime until proven guilty beyond a reasonable doubt. But the conviction of Blaise – twice – for Bailey's murder, illustrates that it is not so much a legal principle, as it is a catchy feel good phrase that can have little meaning in the real world of this country's courtrooms. Blaise's two convictions are proof positive that a skilled prosecutor standing before a jury pointing an accusatory finger at a defendant can overcome an absence of incriminating evidence.

That is why the world is still waiting to be shown something, anything, that rises to the level of convincing evidence and not mere unsubstantiated speculation, that Duran Bailey was murdered by Kirstin Blaise Lobato.

| Key dates of events in the intertwining of Kirstin Blaise Lobato's life and Duran Bailey's death ||
Date	Event
May 25, 2001 [2]	A "really big" African-American who was "huge" compared to 18-year-old Kirstin "Blaise" Lobato attempts to rape her after midnight in the parking lot of a Budget Suites hotel in east Las Vegas. The 5'-6" Blaise escapes after stabbing one time at her attacker's exposed groin with a butterfly knife she carries for self-protection. The man is alive and attempting to get up as she flees in her car.
July 2, 2001	Blaise drives her red Fiero to Panaca, 170 miles north of Las Vegas in Lincoln County. She parks her car on the public street in front of her parent's house where she stays with her dad, stepmother and younger sister.
July 8, 2001	5'-10" and 137 pound Duran Bailey is beaten and stabbed to death inside the trash enclosure for a west Las Vegas bank. [3] After he dies his penis is severed, his body is wrapped in plastic and trash is heaped on his body to conceal it. After a dumpster diver discovers Bailey's body, Las Vegas Metropolitan Police Department detectives Thomas Thowsen and James LaRochelle are assigned to investigate the case.
July 9, 2001	Diann Parker, who reported being raped by Bailey on July 1, 2001, and who lives less than 100 yards from Bailey's murder scene, is informally questioned by Thowsen and LaRochelle.
July 9, 2001	Blaise returns to Las Vegas with her friend Doug Twining, who drove to Panaca to pick her up.
July 13, 2001	Blaise returns to Panaca with her dad, who drove to Las Vegas to pick her up.
July 20, 2001	Lincoln County Juvenile Probation Officer Laura Johnson telephones the Las Vegas police and tells Thowsen third-hand gossip that Blaise may have severed a man's penis during an attempted rape in Las Vegas. Thowsen decides Blaise murdered Bailed based on what Johnson tells him.
July 20, 2001	In the afternoon Thowsen, LaRochelle and a crime scene analyst drive to Panaca to arrest Blaise for Bailey's murder. Her car is towed to Las Vegas to be examined for possible crime scene evidence.
July 23, 2001	Charge of first-degree murder with a deadly weapon filed by the Clark County District Attorney. The D.A. reserves the option to seek the death penalty against Blaise.
July 31, 2001	D.A files amended charges that includes necrophilia (sexual penetration of a dead human body) based on the coroner's report that the sharp object used to slice Bailey's rear-end also cut his anus.
Late July 2001	The Las Vegas Metro PD crime lab finds no evidence in Blaise's car and it is released to her father.
August 7, 2001	Blaise is held over for trial after a preliminary hearing. Her bail is set at $32,000.
May 19, 2002	Blaise is convicted by a jury of first-degree murder with a deadly weapon and sexual penetration of a dead human body. She is sentenced to a minimum of 40 years in prison before she is eligible for parole.
September 3, 2004	Blaise's convictions are overturned and her retrial is ordered by the Nevada Supreme Court.
December 2005	Blaise is released pending her retrial on $500,000 bail posted by her supporters.
October 6, 2006	Blaise is convicted by a jury of voluntary manslaughter with a deadly weapon and sexual penetration of a dead human body. Blaise's bail is revoked and she is immediately taken into custody.
February 2, 2007	Blaise is sentenced to a minimum of 13 years in prison before she is eligible for parole.
December 2007	Blaise's appeal brief is filed with the Nevada Supreme Court.

I
Homeless Man Murdered Near The Las Vegas Strip

Las Vegas was hot and arid on the evening of Sunday, July 8, 2001. A man looking for dumpsters to rummage through was walking several blocks west of the city's world famous casino and hotel Strip around 10:15 p.m., when he noticed that the gate to a trash enclosure in a bank's parking lot was unlocked. Looking inside he saw there wasn't much garbage in the dumpster, but it was cocked and he saw a lot of garbage piled behind it. He went behind the dumpster and after moving a bag he saw a sneaker. He then raised a piece of cardboard and saw the leg of what he was able to identify was a "black person's body." [4] He immediately walked to a gas station less than 100 yards away and called 911 from a payphone. He reported finding a body in the trash enclosure on the parking lot of the Nevada State Bank near the intersection of West Flamingo and Arville. [5] The emergency call was received at 10:36 p.m., and a police car was dispatched to the scene. [6]

Police at crime scene

The first police officers arrived at about 10:50 p.m. [7] One of the officers, James Testa, went inside the trash enclosure and saw a human foot exposed with the rest of the person's body buried under a pile of trash. [8] Emergency services was called after the person didn't verbally respond to Testa.. He also saw still moist bloody shoeprints leading away from the body toward the trash enclosure's opening.

After medical personnel arrived, one of them lifted the trash covered cardboard and determined the body was that of a dead man. The officers then proceeded from the assumption that the dead man was the victim of foul play and sealed off the trash enclosure with crime scene tape.

Several crime scene analysts arrived and they began systematically removing piece by piece the large number of trash items covering the body. Although it was known that one or more persons was likely involved in the man's demise, and they likely touched each item covering his body, only a few items were collected as evidence – while the rest of the evidence was discarded.

When the body was fully uncovered in the early morning hours of Monday, July 9, it was apparent that the man had many wounds, including an amputated penis. There was an area in the back left corner of the enclosure next to his body where blood from his injuries had collected. Clear plastic was wrapped around his body, and white paper towels were stuffed where his penis had been. Although the paper towels were presumably handled by Bailey's assailant(s), they were among the discarded evidence.

From the personal effects found in the trash enclosure, it appeared that was where the man had been living.

It wasn't until 3:50 a.m. on Monday the 9th, that the coroner's investigator examined the body at the scene. She determined there was no significant degree of decomposition, and he was in full rigor mortis. At 8.p.m. that night the FBI identified the dead man as Duran Bailey from his fingerprints. [9]

Duran Bailey's foot is visible in the middle, upper right. The rest of his body was found covered in loose trash.

When Shott was questioned at the scene, he said he didn't step in any blood. His shoes were examined and there was no blood on their soles, so he was excluded as making the bloody shoeprints observed by the first officer on the scene (Testa). [10]

Autopsy determines Bailey's cause of death was "blunt head trauma"

Clark County Chief Medical Examiner Lary Simms performed Bailey's autopsy at noon on July 9. He found that while alive, Bailey experienced a plethora of serious injuries to his neck, face, head and upper body, including defensive wounds to his arms and right hand. According to the autopsy report Bailey's injuries included: stab wounds on the front and right front of his neck – which severed his carotid artery; a 4-1/2″ long slash wound on the back of his neck; abrasions and contusions on the left and right side of his face; a bloody nose; multiple lacerations of his lips; a stab wound on his chin and the right side of his forehead; gouges around both eyes; fractures on both his upper and lower jaw; slash wounds on his left chest and left shoulder; four stab wounds in his lower rib cage area; multiple wounds to his lower left and right arm and hand (typically known as defensive wounds); a fractured skull; and six of his teeth were knocked out. Simms also determined that following Bailey's death his anus area was stabbed and sliced at least three inches deep – to his scrotum, and he was stabbed several times in his abdomen, and his penis was severed at its base. [11]

Trash removed from on top of Duran Bailey's body.

Bailey was 5′-10″ and weighed 133 pounds. Simms determined his cause of death was "blunt head trauma," and "a significant contributing condition was multiple stab and incised wounds," including a severed carotid artery. [12]

Medical Examiner Simms estimates Bailey's time of death

A month after Bailey's autopsy, Simms expressed his opinion during a preliminary hearing for the person charged with Bailey's murder that it was "more likely than not" his death occurred within 12 hours from the time his body was discovered on the evening of Sunday, July 8. [13]

Bailey's time of death could have been significantly narrowed if the "potassium eye fluid test" had been conducted. Simms testified at the preliminary hearing on August 7, 2001, that the test could aid in more accurately estimating Bailey's time of death, but he had not been requested to perform the test. [14] Public

Trash enclosure where Bailey was murdered.

Nevada State Bank

defender Phil Kohn asked Simms on cross-examination, "Is that test still available to us?", to which Simms responded, "Yes." [15] Kohn, however, did not pursue having the test performed.

Internationally known forensic pathologist and author Dr. Michael M. Baden has described how the "potassium eye fluid test" is used as a reliable way to determine a person's time of death: "The test measures changes in the level of potassium in the eye fluid. In life, there is a small amount of potassium in the eye fluid. After death the red cells break down, and the potassium in them enters the vitreous fluid very slowly. The level rises predictably. This happens regardless of temperature." [16] So exposure of Bailey's body to Las Vegas' July heat wouldn't affect the test's outcome.

As of November 2007, the "potassium eye fluid test" that could more accurately identify the time range of when Bailey's death occurred has not been performed. The failure to perform that test would prove to have serious consequences for the person LVMPD detectives soon tagged for Bailey's brutal murder, and the near ritualistic like sexual mutilation of his body after his death.

Non-investigation of prime suspects

Las Vegas Metropolitan Police Department (LVMPD) Homicide Detectives Thomas Thowsen and James LaRochelle were assigned to investigate the case. They arrived at the scene while the crime scene investigators were still working, and they interviewed Shott at 1:23 a.m.

Thowsen and LaRochelle immediately had a prime suspect. While the crime scene was still being processed on the morning of July 9, a woman named Diann Parker approached one of the police officers before 6 a.m. and told him, 'I might know who that guy is. I was the victim of a rape a week ago and that might be the guy that did it.' The information was promptly relayed to the detectives. They checked and verified that only days before Bailey's murder Parker had reported being brutally beaten and raped by Bailey.

The detectives went to Parker's apartment later that morning to informally question her. She lived in the Grand View Apartments, the southern edge of which was only about 200 feet north of the Nevada State Bank. [17] They didn't tape record a statement from her. She told them that Bailey and her were acquaintances. She also said he was a crack cocaine user and she had on occasion exchanged sex with him for crack cocaine that he bought. She said that her roommate Stephen King had heard about a man's murder on the radio, and that is why she went to where Bailey's body was found and asked about him that morning.

During their conversation Parker said that on July 1 while drinking beer in the apartment of several "Mexican" men living in her complex, Bailey barged in and "slapped" her "real hard" and threatened her in the presence of the men. [18] The Mexicans talked with Bailey and told him to leave Parker alone. When she left, they were "watching" to make sure she got back to her apartment safely. Later that day Bailey returned and surprised Parker while she was returning to her apartment from the complex's laundry room. He became enraged when she told him she didn't want anything more to do with him. After forcing his way into her apartment he beat and kicked her, and raped and tried to sodomize her while holding a knife to her neck and throat and threatening to kill.

Afraid to go to the police because of Bailey's threats, she did call 911 three days later, on July 4, when he returned and tried to break into her apartment. She reported the rape and beating to the officer who responded the next day.

She told the officer that reporting Bailey's assault and rape of her was going "to get me killed." She also told the police, "If you all don't catch him, I will be dead." [19] She asked the officer for protection, but instead of offering her police protection he told

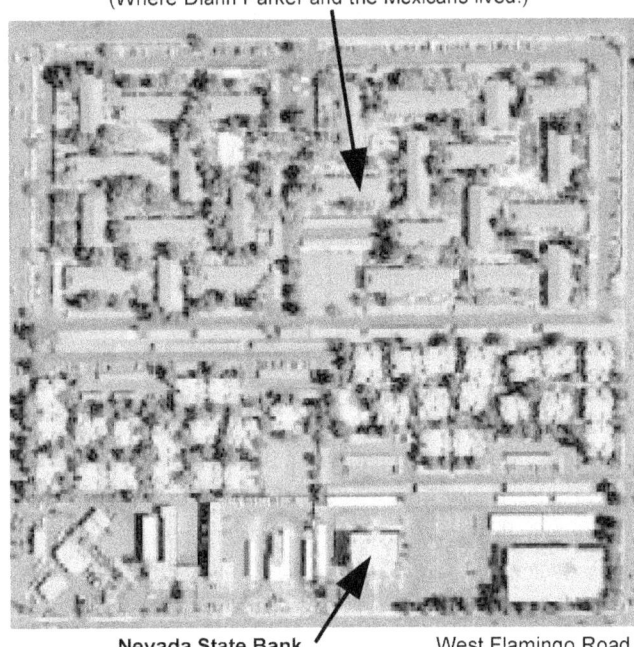

Grand View Apartments
(Where Diann Parker and the Mexicans lived.)

Nevada State Bank
(About 200 feet directly south of the Grand View Apartments, in the same block.)

West Flamingo Road

Duran Bailey's mugshot on October 18, 1999

her, "you got to do what you got to do to protect yourself the best you can." [20] She was reluctant to give him too much information about the Mexicans because she thought they could have been in the country illegally.

Parker also told the officer the homeless Bailey "stayed behind the ... Nevada State Bank" at west "Flamingo and Arville." [21] That is where Bailey's body was found three days later.

The officer took Parker to Las Vegas' University Medical Center where her many injuries and bruises were photographed.

During Parker's conversation with Thowsen she told him the two apartment numbers where the Mexican's lived. He talked with the apartment complex's manager and learned the names they used to rent the apartments. The manager also told him the men didn't cause any trouble. Thowsen ran a criminal background check on the names. No record showed up for any of them so he did not interview the Mexicans, even though based on what Parker said, it was possible no criminal record showed up during his records search because they were illegals using false names. Thowsen did not keep a record of the names and he did not document them in a report.

Thowsen and LaRochelle not only knew that Parker had a significant motive to want to see Bailey harmed or killed, but she appeared at the scene the morning of July 9 after being told a man had been murdered in the area.

Additionally, the photographs of Parker's extensive injuries from the beating Bailey inflicted and his knife wielding were eerily similar to the wounds about Bailey's face and neck. Bailey even cut her neck with the knife near her carotid artery, just as he was cut by his murderer. [22] Also casting suspicion on Parker's possible involvement was her known relationship with Bailey, since Thowsen and LaRochelle would know as homicide detectives that more than three out of four murders involve people acquainted with each other. [23]

In spite of the strong circumstantial evidence suggesting Parker and/or the Mexicans may have been involved in Bailey's murder, Thowsen and LaRochelle didn't pursue interrogating them or obtaining warrants to search their apartments and vehicles to look for the murder weapon(s), bloody shoes or clothing, or any other possibly incriminating physical evidence that could link them to the crime. Neither did they pursue obtaining the phone records of Parker or the Mexicans, or interview any alleged alibi witnesses to verify her and the Mexicans whereabouts on July 8. Neither did the detectives obtain any fingerprint, DNA or blood samples, or shoeprint or vehicle tire tread samples from Parker or the Mexicans to compare with the evidence recovered from the crime scene. That crime scene evidence included fingerprints, bloody shoeprints, tire tread impressions, and biological samples that would be expected to include the killer's DNA.

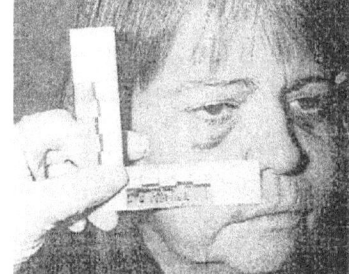
Diann Parker after she reported Duran Bailey raped, beat and threatened to kill her on July 1, 2001 – seven days before he was murdered.

Compounding the detectives failure to investigate Parker or the Mexicans, was they failed to investigate other friends of Parker who might have known and been upset about Bailey's savage physical and sexual assault and death threats against her.

Furthermore, Bailey had lived in the same Grand View Apartments complex as Parker up until a year and a half before his murder. [24] The extensive bruises about her face and neck were clearly visible for days after Bailey's attack, so everyone who saw her knew she had been severely assaulted by fists and possibly an object.

In spite of that, Thowsen did not even attempt to conduct an investigation to obtain information about possible enemies that Bailey may have had in the apartment complex who knew about his attack of Parker.

On July 23, Thowsen went back and took a taped statement from Parker about what she told him on July 9. However, he didn't take her statement as a suspect, but as a person with personal knowledge about Bailey.

Thowsen and LaRochelle knew that Parker and/or her acquaintances had the motive, means and opportunity to murder Bailey. Yet, even though there was considerable circumstantial evidence suggesting a strong connection between Parker's rape and beating and the manner of Bailey's death, they offhandedly dismissed her or anyone she may have known, or anyone who knew Bailey had raped and beaten her, as a possible murder suspect after conducting what cannot even be called a superficial investigation. [25] When asked later why he did not interview the Mexicans after talking with Parker on July 9, Thowsen said words to the effect, 'It was a long day and we were getting tired and at some point you just have to call it a day.'

The consequences of Thowsen and Rochelle's failure to investigate any of the leads connected to Bailey's alleged beating and rape of Parker, and the failure to pursue obtaining fingerprint, shoeprint, and DNA samples from the Mexicans to compare with the crime scene evidence, would become apparent when on July 20 they arrested a young woman for Bailey's murder.

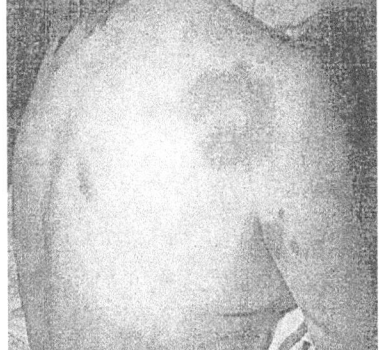

Bruises on Diaan Parker's shoulder, right arm and back from Bailey's alleged rape assault on July 1, 2001.

II
Third-hand Information Relied On To Arrest And Charge Kirstin Blaise Lobato With Duran Bailey's Murder

Laura Johnson provides detective with "third-hand" tip about a Las Vegas stabbing

On July 20, twelve days after Bailey's death, Thowsen received a phone call from Laura Johnson, the juvenile probation officer for Lincoln County, Nevada. Johnson's office was in the county seat of Pioche, more than 170 miles north of Las Vegas. Johnson informed Thowsen that Dixie Tienken, a Lincoln County teacher, told her two days earlier that a former student of Dixie's told Dixie that she had cut off the penis of a man who attacked her in Las Vegas. However, Johnson did not say that Dixie was told the man died. Johnson told Thowsen that the young woman's name was Kirstin Blaise Lobato, and she was living with her parents in Panaca, a small town about ten miles southeast of Pioche. (Kirstin goes by, and is known by her middle name, so she will be referred to as "Blaise".) Johnson also told Thowsen she checked and learned that Blaise owned a red 1984 Pontiac Fiero with a custom license plate. Johnson also said that she had a Lincoln County sheriff deputy drive by the home of Blaise's parents, and her Fiero was parked in front on the public street.

Thowsen ran a background check on Blaise after talking with Johnson. He learned she was 18, and that when she was 6-years-old her mother's boyfriend had sexually assaulted her for nine months.

Detectives Thowsen and LaRochelle travel to Lincoln County to arrest Blaise

Thowsen arranged for LaRochelle and crime scene analyst Maria Thomas to travel to Lincoln County, and he called the county sheriff's office to notify them the three would be arriving that afternoon. Thomas was told that she would be impounding a car – Blaise's Fiero. [26]

Within hours after receiving Johnson's phone call, Thowsen, LaRochelle and the crime scene analyst headed north on US Hwy 93 in two vehicles to arrest Blaise for Bailey's murder.

Johnson's statement to Thowsen and LaRochelle

After the nearly three hour drive to Pioche, Johnson gave a taped interview to the detectives. She reiterated what she told Thowsen on the phone. However, she added that the detectives shouldn't contact Dixie – the source of Johnson's third-hand information about what Blaise had allegedly told Dixie – because she thought Dixie would warn Blaise that they were coming to arrest her for murder.

Compounding Johnson's implicating of Blaise in Bailey's murder without any personal knowledge of anything Blaise said, or what she did or didn't do while in Las Vegas, was the fact that Johnson twice made the false declaration in her statement that Blaise had been on probation with Johnson supervising her – after she got into trouble with the law in Lincoln County. [27] As a law enforcement officer Johnson would have known that telling that falsehood to the detectives would inflame them like throwing raw meat to an alligator, and cement their snap assumption that Blaise was Bailey's killer. Contrary to Johnson's assertion, the Lincoln County District Attorney reports that Blaise has never been investigated, arrested, convicted, sentenced, or served any probationary term for any alleged violation of any law in Lincoln County. [28] However, the detectives didn't know the truth because they didn't verify any of the claims Johnson made on the telephone nor during her interview before deciding Blaise was Bailey's murderer. [29]

After arranging for a Lincoln County sheriff's deputy to accompany them to where Blaise was living, and arranging for a flat-bed tow truck to transport her car to Las Vegas, Thowsen and his colleagues headed to nearby Panaca to arrest Blaise.

Thowsen and LaRochelle were unaware the incident Dixie told Johnson about wasn't Bailey's murder

What Thowsen and LaRochelle didn't know before forming their opinion about Blaise's guilt, was that the incident Blaise told Dixie about was an attempted rape that she fended off with a knife six weeks prior to Bailey's July 8 murder. Shortly after midnight on or about May 25, a "really big" black man over 6' and 200 pounds grabbed the 5'-6" and 100 pound Blaise from behind as she got out of her car at the Budget Suites hotel near Sam's Town casino on Vegas' far east side. [30] He threw her onto the ground and as he knelt over her with his pants pulled down, she pulled out a butterfly knife her dad gave her for self-protection and she tried to stab or cut his groin area. She was able to get away from him, and she heard him crying and saw him getting up as she drove off. [31]

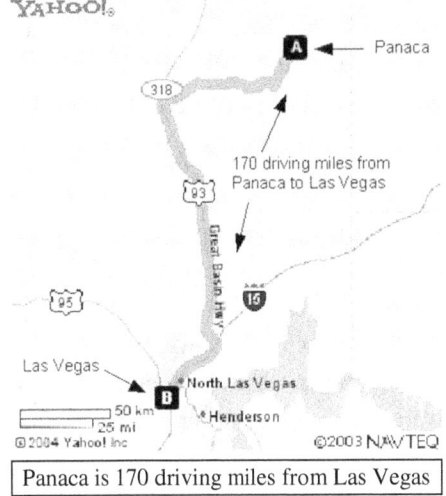

Panaca is 170 driving miles from Las Vegas

If the detectives had conducted even a perfunctory investigation into the details of what Blaise told Dixie, they would have learned that prior to Bailey's murder Blaise had told multiple people about the attack on her that occurred just before the Memorial Day weekend – eight miles from where Bailey was murdered weeks later on Vegas' west side. [32] They also would have learned from a minimal investigation that at least eleven people would swear they saw Blaise in Panaca on July 8 at times from very early in the morning, to throughout the day, to late that evening. The detectives also would have discovered much more evidence, including medical and telephone records, that excluded Blaise from even cursory suspicion of being involved in Bailey's murder.

However, the detectives didn't have any idea they were targeting the wrong person because they decided to arrest Blaise without conducting any investigation whatsoever into the substance of Johnson's conversation with Dixie, who at Johnson's urging they did not interview prior to pursuing Blaise's arrest for Bailey's murder.

Blaise's July 20, 2001 interrogation

When the detectives arrived at the home of Blaise's parents, Larry and Becky Lobato, Blaise was in the shower and they were let in by her younger sister Ashley. Neither of her parents were home. The first thing Thowsen said to Blaise when he began interrogating her was they knew she had been sexually molested by her mother's boyfriend when she was six-years-old. Blaise began sobbing and continued to do so, even after she signed a *Miranda* waiver at 5:55 p.m. [33] Twelve minutes after Blaise signed the waiver Thowsen turned his tape recorder on at 6:07 p.m.

Blaise thought they were interrogating her about the Budget Suites hotel assault in May, because at no time before or after the tape recording began did Thowsen or LaRochelle tell her they were investigating the murder of a man who had been savagely beaten and sexually mutilated, its location in Las Vegas, or the day it happened. Consequently, she had no way of knowing the details of the May assault she told the detectives about bore no relationship whatsoever to the circumstances or details of Bailey's death six weeks later on July 8.

The detectives, however, were aware of many details related to Bailey and his murder. There are at least sixteen significant details in Blaise's 26-minute recorded statement inconsistent with specific details of Bailey's death that Thowsen and LaRochelle would have known at the time of her interrogation and arrest on July 20, 2001. (See, Table 1, p. 17.) The detectives, however, disregarded those many inconsistencies.

There are twelve additional significant details in Blaise's statement inconsistent with the details of Bailey's death that the detectives and the Clark County District Attorney's Office would have been aware of after her arrest, due to forensic testing, expert evidence analysis, or subsequent witness interviews. (See, Table 2, p. 19.) The detectives likewise disregarded those many inconsistencies as they became known.

No matching points between Bailey's murder and Blaise's statement

That Bailey, and Blaise's assailant were black, both events occurred in Las Vegas, and a sharp object was involved, were the only three general areas of intersection between the undisputed circumstances of Bailey's death and Blaise's statement. However, those didn't remotely "match," because Bailey was a smaller man – shorter and much lighter than Blaise's assailant; Bailey was killed eight miles west of where Blaise was assaulted; and Blaise only described trying to cut her assailant's exposed penis once before she was able to get free and flee while he was alive. In contrast Bailey was beaten severely, and stabbed and cut many times while alive, before being beaten, having his penis amputated, and possibly having his anus lacerated after his death. There are thus no actual matching points between Blaise's statement and the specific details of Bailey's death.

Undercutting the suggestion that it is too coincidental to believe that Blaise's fending off a sexual assault by a black man with a knife, and Bailey's stabbing and sexual dismemberment six weeks later are different events, is that in 2001 Las Vegas had more than 52,000 blacks and 7.549 reported violent crimes (3,749 of those reported crimes were rapes or assaults). [34] In addition, the involvement of a knife or other sharp object in a crime is common – even in a murder. According to the FBI, nationally in 2001, 13% of all murders were by a knife or other sharp object, [35] and 17.8% (more than 1 out of 6) of all aggravated assaults involved a knife or other sharp object. [36] So a different black man involved in separate violent crimes involving a sharp object eight miles and six weeks apart, is anything but unusual in Las Vegas, a large city of 84 square miles [37] that experiences more than 20 *reported* violent crimes *per day*, including more than 10 *reported* rapes and assaults *daily*. It is sobering to consider that there were almost 500 rapes and assaults in Las Vegas during the six weeks between the assault Blaise described and Bailey's murder.

Thus, consistent with the principle of Occam's razor – "All things being equal, the simplest solution tends to be the best one." – the most direct and logical explanation for the extreme dissimilarity between Blaise's statement and the details of Bailey's murder is that they were different events.

Underscoring that conclusion is consideration of the principle underlying a technique of fingerprint examination. The number of matching ridge points between two fingerprint samples are identified to determine the likelihood they were made by the same person. In some jurisdictions, such as until recently in England, 16 points had to intersect before a match was declared between a latent crime scene fingerprint and a suspect's print. If the details of Blaise's statement and the details of Bailey's death were considered as constituting separate "fingerprints," and the details of both were individually plotted, Blaise would categorically be rejected as being involved in Bailey's murder.

No confession by Blaise

During their interrogation of Blaise, Thowsen and LaRochelle did not ask her questions directly related to the peculiar facts of Duran Bailey's murder and post-death mutilation. Neither did they ask her questions about its location and the day it occurred, nor did she say anything implicating her in Bailey's murder. Furthermore, at no time after terminating their interrogation did the detectives make any effort to have Blaise write out and sign a confession to Bailey's murder, nor did the detectives make any effort to write a confession for Blaise to sign.

Blaise's arrest

True to the detective's purpose of traveling to Panaca to arrest Blaise on the basis of Johnson's third-hand information, Thowsen and LaRochelle abruptly terminated Blaise's interrogation after she told them she had been attacked "over a month ago," and formally placed her under arrest for the murder of Bailey with a deadly weapon. That her interrogation didn't yield a single incriminating detail, and that the details she provided excluded her from consideration of involvement in Bailey's murder, makes it clear that the naive 18-year-old Blaise's formal arrest was only delayed for a half-an-hour or so by her giving a statement.

Blaise as a high school senior in 2000

[38] Although Thowsen and LaRochelle did not have any corroborative evidence supporting Johnson's implicating of Blaise in Bailey's murder, even if she had been a streetwise girl and asserted her right to the assistance of counsel and to remain silent they would arrested her and hustled her off to Las Vegas. [39]

However, since Blaise wasn't streetwise she also signed several forms consenting to the search of her belongings and her car. The detectives seized the black high-heel shoes she said she was wearing at the time she was assaulted. One of those shoes had a small spot of blood in the big toe area. The spot was later determined to be Blaise's blood, possibly from a blister.

Blaise's car was loaded on the flatbed tow truck to be taken for examination by the LVMPD Crime Lab, and as she was being led to Thowsen's vehicle, her dad Larry arrived after being called at work by her stepmom, Becky. Thinking she was being arrested for fending off the attempted rape in May that she told her dad about when he visited her in Las Vegas in June, she said, "I'm sorry, daddy. I told you I did something awful." Thowsen gave Blaise's dad one of his cards before Thowsen and LaRochelle headed to Las Vegas with Blaise.

Blaise was booked into the Clark County Detention Center that night and three days later, July 23, she was charged with, "murder with use of a deadly weapon." [40] The Clark County District Attorney reserved the option to seek the death penalty. Three days later the DA added the charge that she violated Nevada's necrophilia law ("sexual penetration of a dead human body"), based on ME Simms opinion that Bailey's "anal opening had been cut after his death." [41]

It is indicative of how sloppy, hasty, and incomplete Thowsen and LaRochelle's investigation was that they didn't even know how to correctly spell Blaise's first name before arresting her for Bailey's murder. In her statement they spelled her first name *Kirsten* – not *Kirstin*. They also didn't know at the time they arrested her that when she referred in her statement to returning to Panaca on July 13 from Las Vegas, she had gone there on July 9 – a day after Bailey's death – and that she was in Panaca on the July 8, so she couldn't have murdered him. (See Table 3, p. 57.) However, the detectives didn't know that because they neither asked Blaise to elaborate on her statement, nor did they do any investigation of what she said prior to arresting and whisking her to the county jail in Las Vegas.

Thowsen and LaRochelle conduct superficial investigation after Blaise's arrest

Three days after Blaise's arrest, Thowsen and LaRochelle went back to get a taped statement from Parker to determine her value as a prosecution witness. Blaise's arrest confirmed his snap decision to exclude Parker and her acquaintances as suspects. The detectives also interviewed several acquaintances of Blaise's in Las Vegas.

Six days after Blaise's arrest, Thowsen returned to Lincoln County and interviewed Dixie and several other people. He didn't talk with either of Blaise's parent, her sister Ashley, or other people in the area who had personal knowledge Blaise and her car had been in Panaca on July 8. None of the few people Thowsen talked with implicated Blaise in Bailey's death – not even Dixie.

Dixie's taped statement of Blaise's conversation with her differed in important details from Johnson's claims of what Dixie said Blaise said to her. Particularly, Dixie did not say that Blaise told her she was hiding out, and Dixie did not say her parents were doing anything to hide or get rid of her car, or camouflage it by painting it. Nor did Dixie say that Blaise asked her not to tell anyone about the assault she described. [42] Dixie also told Thowsen and LaRochelle twice that the man who attacked Blaise was alive after she got away from him by trying to stab or cut him, because she saw him "stumbling and getting up" as she was leaving in her car. [43] Dixie told the detectives about her conversation with Blaise, "And, she said I did something and I could have hurt somebody but I'm not sure what all I did, and then she told me that a guy tried to rape her and that she cut off his penis ..." [44] However, Dixie qualified that later when she said that the man's penis may not have been severed because Blaise routinely exaggerates her stories to be more colorful. [45] (A number of people who know Blaise also reported that same trait of hers.) Thowsen immediately terminated his questioning of Dixie after she told him that Blaise saying that she cut off a man's penis couldn't be taken at face value as true. He didn't ask Dixie a single follow-up or additional question.

Prior to Thowsen's termination of the interview, Dixie twice told him that Blaise said the assault happened when it was "dark." [46] Dixie also told Thowsen that Blaise said she had trouble with her car, and that it had "broken down" at least one time in Las Vegas. [47]

Dixie was so certain that when Blaise drove away her attacker was still alive, that Dixie told Thowsen she thought that if Blaise's attacker was married, his biggest problem would be explaining to his wife how he had been injured:

> So, I really thought you know, if this guy was married or something and wouldn't want his wife to know, I mean eventually he would have had to tell her, but if he had a wife, or had anyplace else, I don't think he would have gone to a hospital, he probably would have gone to a doctor, and, and maybe he was able to get it fixed. How do I know?" [48]

Thowsen was somewhat taken aback by Dixie's certainty that the man who attacked Blaise was not only alive, but that she thought his biggest problem would be dealing with his wife, not any wound possibly inflicted by Blaise. Since Thowsen had impulsively arrested Blaise on a murder charge based on what Johnson had said that Dixie had said that Blaise told her, he might have been alarmed to realize that if he had taken the time to confirm what Johnson said by promptly talking to Dixie, he would not have arrested Blaise – and he would have had to eliminate her as a suspect in Bailey's murder.

Dixie told *Justice:Denied* magazine during a January 6, 2007 interview, that when she talked with Johnson she thought Blaise's car was still in Las Vegas, so her parent's couldn't have been trying to hide it or doing anything to camouflage it. Dixie also said Blaise didn't even suggest she was trying to keep the assault secret, which Blaise described as having occurred more than a month prior to their conversation. Dixie also said, consistent with her trial testimony, that she and Blaise performed an Internet search of Las Vegas news stories going back to the first of June for any articles about a man injured by a knife. Dixie also told *Justice:Denied* that Thowsen talked to her for quite some time on July 26, 2001, before turning on his tape recorder. While the tape recorder was off, Dixie said Thowsen tried to pressure her to shape her statement to what he wanted her to say Blaise told her, not what she recollected. [49] Unbeknownst to Dixie at the time, Thowsen was apparently pressuring her so her statement would match Johnson's statement.

The picture painted by Thowsen and LaRochelle's witness interviews *after* Blaise's arrest is their attitude was they were only interested in information consistent with Johnson's statement upon which they based Blaise's arrest and murder charge. Everything else was ignored.

People in Lincoln County learn Bailey was killed when Blaise was in Panaca

The Las Vegas *Review-Journal* published an article on July 25 that reported Blaise was charged with murdering Bailey on July 8. [50] That article was the first that the Lobato family and other people in Panaca knew that July 8 was the date of the incident Blaise was accused of being involved in.

Becky Lobato immediately called the *Review-Journal* and told them they had made a mistake on the date of July 8. She was told it was correct. Blaise's dad Larry then called Thowsen and left a message. When Thowsen returned the call, Larry told him they had charged the wrong person because Blaise had been in Panaca all day on the 8th. Thowsen response was "that as far as he was concerned he had arrested and charged the right person and did not need any further information." [51] Thowsen wasn't interested in "further information" because two days after Blaise's arrest the detectives had completed a report on the LVMPD's investigation of Bailey's murder. [52] Relying on that report, the Clark County DA filed first-degree murder charges against Blaise on July 23, and she was arraigned on July 24, four days after her arrest. During a subsequent phone conversation at the end of July, Larry reiterated that Thowsen had arrested a person who had been almost two hundred miles from Las Vegas when Bailey was murdered. During that contentious conversation Thowsen did agree to authorize the release of Blaise's Fiero, since no evidence tying it to Bailey's murder was discovered after its thorough examination by the LV Metro PD Crime Lab.

> ### Blaise's arrest "is a very peculiar story"
>
> Nationally known forensic psychiatrist Dr. Michael Welner, was interviewed by the Las Vegas *Review-Journal* for its July 25, 2001 article about Blaise's case. Welner said of a woman being accused of mutilating a body, "It is extremely unusual, extremely unusual." He also said, "This is a very peculiar story. It is the kind of thing that just happens in the movies."

Crime lab tests exclude Blaise

Almost a week after Blaise's arrest, and days after she was charged, evidence recovered from the crime scene that included, fingerprints, chewing gum and tire treads, as well as Blaise's car and personal effects, were examined by the LVMPD Crime Lab. Blaise was excluded as the source of four identifiable crime scene fingerprints recovered from the edge of the dumpster enclosure and on items found near Bailey's body. She was also excluded as the source of DNA that wasn't Bailey's which was recovered from a piece of chewing gum found on the cardboard covering Bailey's body, and which had his blood on it. A metal baseball bat with a porous rubber handle that Blaise kept in her car for self-defense tested negative for the presence of blood. A spot on the interior of her car's driver's side door panel and on her car seat cover tested weakly positive after a presumptive luminol test for the presence of an unknown iron bearing substance (blood contains iron), but both spots tested negative as being blood when subjected to a precise confirmatory test. The presumptive luminol test reactions in Blaise's car were not unusual since numerous natural and man-made substances will trigger a false positive when looking for blood traces – which is why a confirmatory test is mandatory.

Somewhat remarkably, the single most important piece of evidence recovered from the crime scene – Bailey's severed penis that was handled by his killer, or at least one of his killers – wasn't tested for the presence of identifiable foreign DNA before being buried with his body.

The crime lab did not analyze the bloody shoeprints leading away from Bailey's body, so Blaise's public defenders retained a nationally renowned shoeprint expert, William J. Bodziak. A former FBI crime lab technician, Bodziak wrote in his report of March 27, 2002:

> Based on the corresponding dimensions of comparable portions of other brands of footwear having this generic design, it was determined the Q1-Q2 impressions most closely correspond to a U.S. men's size 9 athletic shoe of this type. The American women's size equivalent would be approximately size 10.

> … Using a standard Brannock foot-measuring device, the length of the LOBATO right foot equates to U.S. men's sizes between 6 to 6-1/2. The American women's size equivalent would be approximately size 7-1/2. The right foot size of KIRSTIN LOBATO would therefore be at least 2-1/2 sizes smaller than the estimated crime scene shoe size.

> Based on these observations and significant size differences, it was determined that the Q1-Q2 crime scene impressions are from considerably larger shoes than the size that would accommodate LOBATO's feet. [53]

Location of Bailey's murder in west Las Vegas and Blaise's assault in east Last Vegas

Nevada State Bank
Scene of Bailey's murder
(West Las Vegas)

Budget Suites Hotel
Scene of Blaise's attempted rape
(East Las Vegas)

8 miles

East Las Vegas

Jeremy Davis' house
Where Blaise went to get cleaned up after being attacked (less than a mile from the Budget Suites)

Table 1
16 Significant Differences Between Bailey's Death and Blaise's Statement Known to the LVMPD at the Time of Her Arrest on July 20, 2001 [54]

Difference	Bailey	Blaise
Date	Bailey was murdered on July 8, 2001.	Blaise specifically described the attack occurred "over a month ago," from the date of the July 20 interrogation – or prior to June 20. [55] Other details she and Jeremy Davis provided pinpoint it to on or about May 25, 2001.
Location	Bailey's murder occurred on the west side of Las Vegas – a few blocks from the Vegas strip that demarcates east and west Las Vegas.	Blaise described a rape attempt that occurred on the far east side of Las Vegas near the intersection of Boulder Hwy and S. Nellis Blvd. (Eight miles east of Bailey's murder.) Consistent with that location is Blaise said she immediately went to her friend Jeremy Davis' house and cleaned herself up. Davis' house is about 1 mile from the Budget Suites Hotel, and 8 miles from the Nevada State Bank.
Place	Bailey was murdered inside of the trash enclosure for a Nevada State Bank.	Blaise described being assaulted in the parking lot of a Budget Suites Hotel.
Geography	There was no shopping center across the street from where Bailey was murdered, there was no fountain visible from the Bank's parking lot, and there was no Sam's Town casino nearby.	Blaise provided specific details about the area around where she was assaulted, including the shopping center across the street, the Budget Suites' fountain, and that it was near Sam's Town casino.
Physique	Bailey was 5'-10" and weighed 133 lbs. (at time of autopsy). (Bailey lost approximately 40% of his blood (two quarts), which would have weighed approx. 4 lbs. So his pre-death weight was about 137 lbs.) [56]	The 5'-6" Blaise described her assailant as "really big," and "he seemed like a giant compared to me" when she was standing next to him before he threw her on the ground. (Consistent with her initial description, Blaise assailant was later described as over 6' and 200 lbs.[57])
Attack	Bailey was viciously pummeled, stabbed, slashed, and after dying his abdomen was stabbed, his penis was severed at its base, and his anus was cut with an unidentified sharp object.	Blaise described stabbing one-time at her attackers exposed groin area with a butterfly knife. (She later said the knife was given to her by her father for self-defense.)
Condition	Bailey was dead when his attacker(s) left.	Blaise described her attacker as "crying" when she got away from him.
Circumstances	Bailey was killed in an altercation that occurred entirely in the back of the trash enclosure where he was living.	Blaise described being bum rushed when she got out of her car in the Budget Suites parking lot. At no time did she describe that the ensuing struggle occurred inside a trash enclosure.
Drugs	Bailey was a crack cocaine user who was not known to use methamphetamines, and had cocaine in his system at the time of his death.	Blaise described using methamphetamines continuously for a week before and after being attacked. (It was later learned that Blaise's mother took her to a doctor in Caliente on July 5, and her blood drawn at 5:15 p.m. tested negative for the presence of methamphetamines.)
Striking	Bailey's cause of death was "blunt head trauma," according to the autopsy performed on July 9, 2001, and he had numerous pummeling type injuries.	Blaise said, "No," she didn't remember hitting her assailant a single time. (Consistent with that is Blaise had no bruises, cuts, broken bones or any other injuries to either of her hands.)

Table 1 (Continued)

Difference	Bailey	Blaise
Dumpster	Bailey was murdered inside of a trash enclosure directly next to a dumpster.	Blaise described being assaulted in an open "parking lot" and "there was a dumpster not far from where it happened."
Curb	There are indications the car that left the tire tracks next to the trash enclosure drove over a planter median.	Blaise stated she didn't drive over "anything" when she drove away.
Covered Body	Bailey was wrapped in plastic, covered by a piece of cardboard with bloody shoeprints imprinted on it, and then a large quantity of trash was heaped on him.	Blaise stated "No," she didn't cover her assailant with anything, she immediately got in her car and drove away while he was "crying."
Dragging Body	Bailey appeared to have been dragged a very short distance (1'-2') from the left rear corner of the trash enclosure toward the dumpster.	Blaise stated "No," she didn't move her assailant at all.
Hygiene	Bailey's aunt who positively identified his body, described him as fastidiously clean, and his shoes were found neatly arranged in an undisturbed part of the trash enclosure. He frequented the nearby Nevada State Bank daily, and no prosecution witness familiar with Bailey described him as unclean or "smelly."	Blaise described her assailant as "very smelly, ...Like old alcohol and dirty diapers almost." [58]
Behavior	Bailey was known, from the interview with Diann Parker, to exchange crack cocaine for sex.	Blaise did not describe exchanging sex for methamphetamines. (And no evidence has been presented that she ever did so.)

Physical landmarks identified by Blaise in her statement as being near the scene of the attempted rape of her

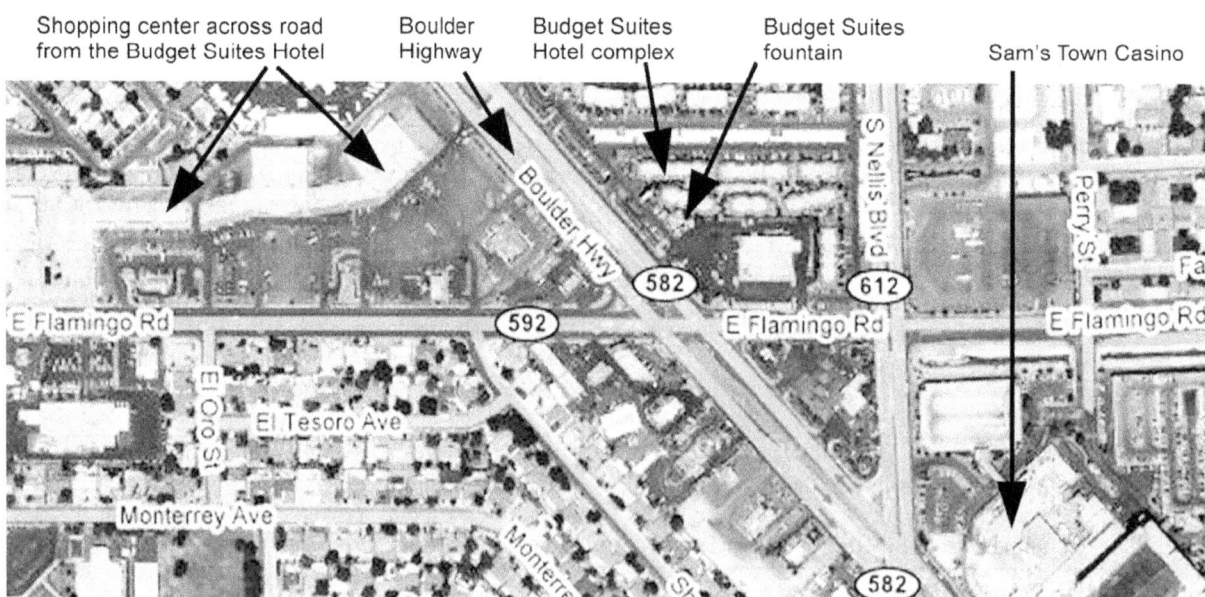

Table 2
12 Significant Differences Between Bailey's Death and Blaise's Statement Learned by the LVMPD and the Clark County D.A.'s Office After July 20, 2001

(Due to forensic testing, expert evidence analysis, or a witness interview after Blaise's arrest.)

Difference	Bailey	Blaise
Sexual Component	A prosecution and defense expert agreed that Bailey's assault and sexual mutilation had a distinct homosexual component.	Blaise is a woman and she was alone when assaulted. Yet, the prosecution has never alleged that anyone other than Blaise was involved in Bailey's death.
Object	Bailey was murdered by an unknown object that experts have variously described as possibly scissors, or a knife with at least a 6″ blade (ME Simms' estimate).	The butterfly knife had a 3-1/2″ - 4″ blade, [59] that Blaise said she used to fend off her attacker.
Shoe Size	The bloody shoeprints leading away from Bailey's body were made by a U.S. man's size 9 athletic shoe, [60] which equals a woman's size 10-1/2.	Blaise wears a woman's size 7-1/2 that equates to a U.S. man's size 6, which is 3 sizes smaller than the bloody shoeprints. [61] The black high-heel shoes that Blaise said she was wearing when assaulted tested negative for the presence of blood on their soles.
Shoe Type	The bloody shoeprints leading away from Bailey's body were made by a man's size 9 athletic shoe. [62]	Blaise described wearing "black high heels." [63] Those black high heels were seized at the time of Blaise's arrest. The heels neither matched the bloody shoeprints, nor did they have blood on their sole. That Blaise was wearing high heels is consistent with her statement that when she was attacked, "I was getting ready to go out." [64]
Bat	ME Simms and a defense expert determined it was not probable that any of Bailey's injuries were caused by a baseball bat.	Blaise described keeping a baseball bat in her car for self-defense, which later tested negative for the presence of blood or other biological material.
Blood Pool	Bailey had numerous bleeding wounds and there was a pool of blood where he bled.	Blaise described herself as lying down as her assailant knelt on top of her. If he had been profusely bleeding, or she had been laying in a pool of his blood, she would have been bathed in his blood and transferred it to numerous areas of her car, including the exterior driver's side door handle, the steering wheel, head rest, floor board, foot pedals, seat, seat back, etc. Scientific confirmatory tests were negative for the presence of any blood on the interior or exterior of her car.
Tire Tracks	The tire tread design of the undisturbed tire tracks near the trash enclosure were identified.	Blaise described driving away from her assailant in her car, which had a different tread design than the tire tracks found at the scene of Bailey's murder. That is consistent with the numerous people who testified about their personal observation that Blaise's car had not been driven from where it was parked in front of her parents Panaca home from July 2, 2001, to the time it was seized by the LVMPD on July 20, 2001.
Drug Use	Bailey had crack cocaine in his system when he died.	Blaise only described using methamphetamines and her use of the drug was later verified by acquaintances and family members. She did not say she used cocaine, and no one reported that she used cocaine.
Blood Dripping	Bailey's blood did not drip vertically from his wounds in the opinion of two experts – so he was stabbed in a prone position.	Blaise only described stabbing once at her assailant as he was above her while *she* was lying on the ground.

Table 2 (Continued)

Difference	Bailey	Blaise
Date Mismatch	Bailed was killed on July 8, 2001.	Blaise said that she was assaulted more than a month before the July 20 interrogation, and that for a week before and a week after the assault "I was out of my mind on drugs." [65] She also said that the attack on her was at the end of being up for "three days" continuously. [66] Which means that for her to have been assaulted by Bailey, she had been doing meth since July 1 and had not had any sleep since the night of Wednesday, July 4. Blaise returned to Panaca from Las Vegas on July 2, 2001. After her arrest, people who saw her described her as lethargic and sleeping a lot – including during the Fourth of July gathering of family and friends at her parent's house. On July 5, three days before Bailey's death, Blaise's mom took her to the Caliente Clinic where a blood sample was drawn at 5:15 p.m. The lab test showed there was no methamphetamines in her system. [67] The doctor requested that Blaise provide a 24-hour urine sample, which was collected by her mom on the morning of the 7th. Blaise's mom stayed home from work to be with her on the 6th. On July 8, at least eleven people (have testified they) saw Blaise in Panaca between 12:30 a.m. and midnight (23-1/2 hours), and none reported (testified) that she either had the appearance of being under the influence of any drugs or of having been awake for days on end. In addition to the negative blood test on the late afternoon of July 5, not a single witness testified to seeing Blaise use, or exhibit any signs of using any drugs of any kind from the time of her arrival in Panaca on July 2 to the time she left on July 9.
Likely Time of Death	ME Simms testified at Blaise's August 2001 preliminary hearing that it was "more likely than not" his death occurred within 12 hours from when the first officer arrived at the scene – or between 10:50 p.m. and 10:50 a.m. on Sunday, July 8. Darkness on July 8 was 9:06 p.m. Thus Simms' estimate encompassed the daylight hours from 10:50 a.m. to 9:06 p.m., and 1-1/2 hours of darkness. During Blaise's retrial Simms testified that to a "medical certainty" Bailey died between 9:50 a.m. and 3:50 p.m. – all daylight hours.	Blaise described twice in her statement being attacked when it was dark, "late at night like probably more into early morning." [68] Since she said she "was getting ready to go out," it could have been from around midnight to 1 a.m., give or take possibly an hour – which would have been 2 a.m. at the outside. Because it was dark, she could only describe her assailant as "black," "big," and "smelly."
Most Remote Time of Death Bailey's Discovery or Examination at Crime Scene	ME Simms testified at Blaise's August 2001 preliminary hearing that it was "more likely than not" his death occurred within 12 hours from when the first officer arrived at the scene. That was about 10:50 p.m., so Bailey's most remote time of death was 10:50 a.m. At Blaise's May 2002 trial Simms testified the latest possible time of Bailey's death was 4:50 a.m., and at her retrial he testified the latest possible time was 3:50 a.m., although to a "medical certainty" it was 9:50 a.m. Dawn on July 8 was 4:24 a.m., so Simms' estimates during the preliminary hearing and Blaise's first trial were Bailey's most remote possible time of death was after dawn, while at Blaise's retrial it was 34 minutes before dawn.	Blaise described twice in her statement being attacked when it was dark, "late at night like probably more into early morning." [69] Since she said she "was getting ready to go out," it could have been from around midnight to 1 a.m., give or take possibly an hour – which would have been 2 a.m. at the outside.

III

Blaise Charged With Violating Nevada's Necrophilia Law Without Any Evidence Bailey's Murderer Had Sex With His Corpse

Several days after Blaise was charged with Bailey's first-degree murder with a deadly weapon, she was also charged with violating Nevada's necrophilia law (NRS 201.450). Understanding the necrophilia law's origin and intended scope is necessary to determine its applicability to the circumstances of Bailey's murder.

In 1982 a seven-year-old girl's corpse was stolen from a mortuary in Nevada's Washoe County (Reno). After the thief had sex with the corpse, he deposited it in a garbage can. After the alleged perpetrator's arrest, prosecutors discovered there was no necrophilia (sex with a corpse) law in Nevada, and that the state's sexual assault law only applies to a living "person," so it was inapplicable to the dead girl's rape.

Necrophilia law introduced

The Washoe County District Attorney responded by drafting a bill criminalizing necrophilia. The Nevada District Attorney Association co-sponsored the bill. Designated A.B. 287, the bill was introduced in the Nevada Assembly on March 2, 1983, and it was summarized as "Prohibits necrophilia." [70]

Ed Basl represented the Washoe County District Attorney's Office, and in his testimony on March 16, 1983 before the Assembly Judiciary Committee, he made it clear that the purpose of the bill was to criminalize the rape of a corpse. Basl specifically stated that the drafter of the bill and its sponsors wanted "to have the penalty the same as a sexual assault [of a live person]." [71] The proposed law was predicated on the assumption that since a dead person (regardless of age) can't provide consent, then any sexual activity with a corpse is non-consensual, and thus the equivalent of raping a live person. [72]

On March 30, 1983 the Nevada Assembly passed the bill.

Basl reiterated during his testimony before the Senate Judiciary Committee on April 5, 1983, that the sole purpose of the bill was to criminalize sexual relations with a corpse: "Mr. Basl went on to say that he does not believe the bill needs to be amended by adding a series of other felony and/or other offenses: that part of the problem as far as the way dead bodies are handled, is covered already by existing legislation, but *the one area that is completely void of mention is the area of sexual assaults being committed on dead bodies.*" [73] Basl testified before the Senate committee, as he had before the Assembly committee, that the sponsors seeking to criminalize necrophilia wanted "to make the penalty conform to those for sexual assault [of a live person]." [74]

The Nevada Senate passed the bill on April 13, 1983. The governor signed the bill on April 20, and it became effective on July 1, 1983. [75]

Legislative intent of the necrophilia law

The only testimony before the House and Senate Judiciary Committees was by Basl. His explanation of the law's intent is unquestionable because he was the official representative of the necrophilia law's drafter and co-sponsor – the Washoe County District Attorney's Office. There was no testimony whatsoever that the law has any application to any situation other than a person engaging in sexual activity with a corpse, which is why it is known as the necrophilia law. The limited scope of the law's applicability is explained by Basl's testimony before the Senate committee that the law was intended to fill the absence of a law prohibiting "sexual assaults being committed on dead bodies." [76]

Basl's testimony of the laws intended purpose is consistent with the crime that inspired the necrophilia law – the rape of a dead young girl's body.

That the necrophilia law was intended to criminalize sex acts with a corpse that would be illegal if performed on a non-consenting (or underage) living person is not only made clear from Basl's testimony before both the Assembly and Senate Judiciary Committees, and the facts of the corpse rape that inspired the law, but from the language of the law itself. It criminalizes "sexual penetration" of a dead body, and it states that "means cunnilingus, fellatio or any intrusion, however slight, of any part of a person's body or any object manipulated or inserted by a person into the genital or anal openings of the body of another, including, without limitation, sexual intercourse in what would be its ordinary meaning if practiced upon the living." [77] Thus insertion of a dildo into a corpse's anus or vagina would be as punishable as the equivalent of doing the same in an illegal manner with a live person.

The intent of the necrophilia law to criminalize the sexual assault of a dead body is further supported by the fact that the definition of "sexual penetration" is almost identical for both the Nevada laws criminalizing "Sexual Assault and Seduction" of a living person and the necrophilia law. [78]

The necrophilia bill's intent as understood from its plain language, Basl's testimony, the circumstances of the dead Washoe County girl's rape, and the legislature's all-encompassing definition of "sexual penetration," is consistent with the *Oxford English Dictionary's* definition of necrophilia: "Fascination with death and dead bodies; esp. sexual attraction to, or intercourse with, dead bodies." [79]

No evidence Bailey was sexually assaulted after he died

At the time the Clark County District Attorney's Office filed the necrophilia charge against Blaise on July 31, 2001, the only evidence of Bailey's injuries was ME Simms' autopsy report that did not state Bailey was sexually assaulted before or after his death. During Blaise's preliminary hearing on August 7, 2001, the DA's Office did not present any eyewitness or expert testimony that Bailey experienced either postmortem anal intercourse or that his penis was used in sexual activity prior to its amputation. What there was during Blaise's preliminary hearing was direct testimony by ME Simms in response to questions by the assistant DA about extensive injuries inflicted on Bailey, which included "slashing" across his rectum/anal area. [80]

Thus Blaise was charged with violating the necrophilia law, and then ordered to stand trial after her preliminary hearing, without any evidence offered by the Clark County DA supporting the allegation that she – or anyone else – had any form of sexual relations with Bailey after his death.

Prosecution alleged injury to Bailey's corpse was violation of necrophilia law

The prosecution justified the necrophilia charge based on Simms' testimony that after Bailey died his anus was slashed by a sharp object. While Simms' testimony may support an accusation of corpse mutilation, it doesn't even support the suggestion, much less a substantive allegation, that Bailey was raped after his death. As Basl made clear in his testimony, the purpose of the necrophilia law was to criminalize the same action inflicted on a corpse that constitutes sexual assault of a live person. Inflicting multiple stabbing and slicing injuries on a living person, including cross-slashing his or her anus, is a form of causing bodily harm. The same is true of the stabbing and slashing wounds inflicted on Bailey's dead body.

So the Clark County District Attorney's Office effectively created an entirely new law never contemplated or enacted by the Nevada Legislature, when it applied the necrophilia law to the facts of Bailey's case. The prosecution did not even allege in charging Blaise with violating the necrophilia law that Bailey's corpse had been raped. Nor did the prosecution allege during Blaise's two trials that Bailey's dead body had been sexually assaulted.

The prosecution wasn't even on completely solid ground in alleging that Bailey's anal injuries were due to slicing by a sharp object. During Blaise's retrial defense medical expert Dr. Michael Laufer testified that in his years as a hospital emergency room physician he had seen many people with anal injuries similar to Bailey's that were caused by the seam of their pants when they were kicked. Thus, in his opinion a sharp object may not have been involved. In spite of their different opinions about the possible cause of Bailey's anal area injury, the common denominator of Simms and Laufer's testimony was that neither opinioned his injury was caused by a person engaging in sex with Bailey's corpse. Likewise, neither opinioned that anyone had sex with Bailey after his death. Consequently, regardless of how Bailey's anal area injury occurred – through a kick to the seam of his pants or by a sharp object – no evidence was presented that the person or persons who murdered him violated the necrophilia law.

The Nevada Supreme Court has only directly addressed the necrophilia law once. In the 1996 case of *Doyle v. State*, the Court ruled that the law's plain meaning, "is to punish the act of sexual penetration of a dead human body, regardless of motive." [81] The Court's ruling in *Doyle v State* concerning motive and the necrophilia law, has no direct applicability to Blaise's case because her alibi defense was she didn't commit the crime. So motive wasn't an issue in her defense.

Even though Bailey wasn't sexually assaulted after his death, the prosecution could be expected to benefit from charging Blaise with violating the necrophilia law. For one thing it transformed her case into being a combination murder and lurid sex crime case, which could psychologically influence the jurors to view the absence of evidence less favorably for her than they otherwise would. The necrophilia charge also provided a means of enhancing Blaise's sentence if she were convicted, by increasing her prison time and requiring her to register as a sex offender upon her release.

Unfortunately for Blaise, her lawyers didn't research the necrophilia law, so they didn't file a motion to dismiss the charge on the basis that the prosecution didn't allege Blaise had sexual relations with Bailey's corpse, and Bailey's anal injury, however it was caused, didn't constitute a violation of the law. [82]

IV
Blaise's May 2002 Trial

Prosecution's lack of evidence solved by jailhouse informant

On the eve of Blaise's trial, ten months after her arrest, the prosecution had no physical, forensic, eyewitness or confession evidence linking her to Bailey's murder. Neither did they have a single witness who saw her or her car in Las Vegas on the day of Bailey's death or for nearly a week preceding it. In contrast, numerous witnesses said she and her car had been in Panaca on July 8 and the six days preceding it, and her presence there was corroborated by medical records, and telephone records of her numerous conversations with Doug Twining, a male friend of hers living in Las Vegas. [83]

What the prosecution did have was a "jailhouse informant" – Korinda Martin. Martin claimed that while they were both in the Clark County Detention Center, Blaise was loudly "bragging" on several occasions in the open area of the jail module (where the prisoners watch television and socialize), "That she was there for murder and that she had cut a man's penis off and stuffed it down his throat." [84] Curiously, the prosecution did not produce any other person – whether a prisoner or jail staff member – claiming to have heard Blaise's alleged loud boasting, that Martin claimed occurred on multiple occasions when a number of people were present. Furthermore, the accurate details about Bailey's murder that Martin claimed Blaise described were included in a July 25, 2001 article about Blaise's arrest in the *Review-Journal*, Las Vegas' most widely read newspaper that was delivered to the jail. While Martin's inaccurate details, such as her claim that Bailey's penis was stuffed in his mouth, were not in the paper.

Blaise's May 2002 trial

Blaise's trial began on May 8, 2002, in the courtroom of Clark County District Court Judge Valorie Vega. Blaise's attorneys were Clark County Public Defenders Gloria Navarro and Phillip Kohn. The prosecutors were Assistant D.A.s Sandra DiGiacomo and William Kephart.

The prosecution tried to influence the jury by generally focusing on a series of prongs that they represented during closing arguments were "proven" by the evidence. The prosecution's case during Blaise's trial can be understood by explaining several of the key prongs the prosecution argued. The following are eight of those prongs, followed by a rebuttal of why each one didn't implicate Blaise in Bailey's murder.

First prosecution prong

It was too coincidental that a knife would be used to stab at a man's groin area in two separate incidents in Las Vegas six weeks apart.

Response

In making that argument, the prosecution ignored that Las Vegas was a crime haven in 2001. According to the FBI's 2001 Uniform Crime Report (UCR), Las Vegas had one of the highest rates of rape in the country, 30% above the national average, [85] and murder was so commonplace that it was double the national average, with almost three per week. [86] Thus, hidden behind the glitzy "fun time" facade of the Las Vegas Strip is the sordid truth that Vegas' "Wild West" crime atmosphere made it one of the most dangerous cities in the country for a young single woman such as Blaise.

Also undermining the prosecution "coincidence" claim is that in 2001 almost two out of five murders were committed by cutting or beating, the causes of Bailey's death. [87]

Consequently, it wasn't unusual for Blaise to use a knife to fend off a sexual assault in late May 2001 in east Las Vegas, and six weeks later for Bailey to be beaten and stabbed to death eight miles away in west Las Vegas. Considering that the details in her July 20, 2001 statement bear no relationship to Bailey's crime scene, but perfectly match the area around the Budget Suites hotel, and those details are consistent with what was going on in her life in May 2001, but not in July, there is no reasonable basis upon which to doubt that Blaise was sexually assaulted in May.

Furthermore, the area around the Budget Suites hotel remains dangerous for a single woman. According to the LVMPD's website, in the 60 days prior to December 23, 2006, there were 116 serious crimes *reported* within a one-half mile radius of the Budget Suites, and 56 of those were assaults. [88] During the same period of time, there were 132 serious crimes *reported* within a one-half mile radius of Bailey's death. [89] So in late 2006 there were an average of more than four serious crimes *reported* every day within 1/2 mile of both locations.

Blaise explained in her statement that she didn't report the May 2001 attack because she had reported previous sexual assaults and the police "basically blew me off. It's been my experience that it doesn't do any good." [90] Blaise had every reason to believe the police would have simply ignored her. She had been repeatedly sexually assaulted when she was six by her mother's boyfriend and nothing of consequence was done to him when it was reported to the police. Then when she was 13 an ex-boyfriend raped her, and a Lincoln County sheriff deputy told her mother and her they would be wasting their time to report it. Then at 17, her best friend's father raped her. None of the three males who had actually raped her had been punished and her attacker of May 2001 didn't actually penetrate her. So why would she bother reporting a violent crime that from her experience the police take a casual attitude toward investigating? In addition to not thinking the police would do anything to pursue her attacker, Blaise didn't have a reason to report the assault because her attacker was visibly alive when she left.

Irrespective of her possible involvement in Bailey's murder, Diann Parker's experience seconded Blaise's opinion that it doesn't do any good to report a rape, by the way the Las Vegas police blew off her report of being savagely beaten and raped by Bailey. Even though Parker had a pulverized face, knife marks on her neck, and bruises all over her body proving Bailey's assault, and she repeatedly expressed fear for her life, the LVMPD didn't even pursue arresting Bailey in spite of being told by her exactly where he lived – about 100 yards from her apartment in the Nevada State Bank's trash enclosure.

Furthermore, Blaise's non-reporting of the May 2001 attempted rape is the *norm*. The U.S. Department of Justice estimates that in 2001 only 39% of rapes and/or sexual assaults nationwide were reported. [91]

Second prosecution prong

The prosecution argued the Budget Suites assault Blaise described and Bailey's murder were the same event.

Response

Blaise's statement did not match the crime scene or the circumstances of Bailey's death. Not the time, the location, the size of her attacker, the type of attack, the injuries involved … nothing. There are at least 28 specific details in her 26-minute statement that are inconsistent with the facts of Bailey's murder. (See Table 1, p. 17, and Table 2, p. 19.)

Third prosecution prong

The prosecution's "theory" of the crime was Bailey's murder resulted from "A drug deal gone bad." [92] The prosecutors speculated in their closing arguments that desperate for methamphetamines to continue the days long binge described in her statement, Blaise drove her Fiero to Las Vegas on July 6, and that early on the morning of July 8 she went to the trash enclosure where Bailey lived to get methamphetamines from him. DiGiacomo further speculated that after Bailey gave Blaise the methamphetamines she didn't want to have sex with him in exchange for them because he was dirty and smelly. Then, because she had been sexually victimized in the past by men, she allegedly reacted violently by beating and stabbing him to death, and after slicing his anus she cut his penis off.

Response

The prosecution's "theory of the crime" was non-fact based speculation for many reasons, including:

• Bailey used crack cocaine, which was in his system at the time of his death, and witnesses testified he didn't use methamphetamines.

• There was no testimony that Bailey ever sold drugs of any kind.

• There was no testimony that Blaise had ever been to the Nevada State Bank, or the bank's parking lot where the trash enclosure Bailey lived in was located.

• There was no testimony that Bailey and Blaise had ever met or otherwise knew of each other.

• There was no testimony that Blaise knew Bailey was living in the trash enclosure.

• Multiple witnesses testified that Blaise used methamphetamines in May and June 2001 when she was staying in Las Vegas, corroborating the methamphetamine use she acknowledged in her statement.

• There was no testimony that Blaise had ever exchanged sex for methamphetamines or any other drug.

• There was no testimony that Blaise or her car was in Las Vegas on July 6, 7 or 8.

• There was no testimony why Blaise would drive 340 miles round-trip from Panaca to Las Vegas solely to get methamphetamines as the prosecution alleged, when it was available within a few minutes of her parent's Panaca house. Thowsen was told by Laura Johnson before Blaise's arrest that drugs were readily available in Lincoln County. [93]

• There was no testimony that Blaise used methamphetamines at any time from when she arrived in Panaca on July 2 until her arrest on July 20.

• A sample of Blaise's blood was drawn for analysis when her mother took her to the doctor in Caliente on July 5. Her blood tested negative for the presence of methamphetamines. [94] Blaise also provided a 24-hour urine sample that was collected on July 7, as a follow-up to help her doctor determine what was ailing her. Blaise's medical records establish she was not on a methamphetamine run during the week prior to Bailey's death, or during the three days, immediately preceding it. That fact, combined with the unrebutted testimony of multiple eyewitnesses and phone records, etc., establishes that Blaise was in Panaca the entire day of Bailey's death.

Fourth prosecution prong

Korinda Martin testified that she met Blaise at the Clark County Detention Center. She claimed that Blaise bragged numerous times about killing Bailey, and that she related "graphic descriptions of how she killed and mutilated" Bailey. [95]

Response

Undermining Martin's claims is that the *accurate* details about Bailey's death that Martin testified Blaise said, were included in a Las Vegas *Review-Journal* article published on July 25, 2001 [96] The inaccurate details Martin testified about weren't reported in the media. That tends to indicate Martin contrived them. Martin claimed e.g., that Blaise boasted she "amputated" Bailey's penis and stuck it "down his throat." [97] Bailey's penis was actually found laying under some trash near his body.

Further undermining the truthfulness of Martin's testimony, is the prosecution didn't produce a single other prisoner or staff member who claimed to have heard on a single occasion, Blaise's alleged jailhouse braggadocio.

Also undermining Martin's testimony is that at the time of Blaise's arrest, Martin was a certified nursing assistant being held at the CCDC awaiting sentencing for her guilty pleas to robbing and coercing one of her patients. [98] Prior to testifying at Blaise's trial, Martin sent several handwritten letters to a former co-prisoner of hers, Brenda Self, requesting that she mail the letters to Martin's sentencing judge. The letters, worded as if they were written by Self, suggested that Martin should be given a lenient sentence so she could be released to care for the wheel-chair bound Self. Copies of those letters, that had been sent to Self in an envelope bearing the CCDC's return address and Martin's prisoner ID number, were provided to Blaise's lawyers prior to her trial. Although the prosecution denied it had made a specific deal with Martin for her testimony, Blaise's lawyers argued outside the jury's presence for admission of the letters to demonstrate Martin's testimony lacked credibility because she was hoping to get a tangible benefit – a sentence reduction – from her testimony against Blaise.

The prosecutors argued the letters should be excluded as evidence, and testimony by Martin and Self about the letters should be barred from the jury, because the letters were "extrinsic." The prosecutors argued the letters had nothing directly to do with the question of Blaise's guilt or innocence. Judge Vega agreed, so the jury wasn't made aware of the letters. [99]

Additional evidence undermining Martin's credibility was discovered *after* Blaise's trial. A Las Vegas police document examiner compared the letter writer's handwriting with that of Korinda Martin. He determined that Martin definitely wrote one of the letters and probably wrote the other letter. [100] Contrary to that finding, Martin had denied under oath that she wrote or mailed the letters. [101] However, when Martin's perjury was brought to the attention of Clark County prosecutors, they didn't pursue her prosecution.

Fifth prosecution prong

The prosecution portrayed Blaise as a killer because she was a bad person of low moral character who grew up in the sticks of Lincoln County, used methamphetamines and on two occasions engaged in amateur exotic dancing in Las Vegas.

Response

Contrary to the prosecution's intimations, there was no testimony supporting that because of her upbringing, experiences or lifestyle, Blaise would ever harm anyone except in self-defense, or that she had ever traded sex for drugs. However, the success of the prosecution's tactic of smearing Blaise, in part because she was from Panaca, was demonstrated when the jurors sent the judge several notes during their deliberations that they were afraid of Blaise's family – who lived in the sticks of Lincoln County. [102]

Sixth prosecution prong

To explain how Bailey's extensive injuries could have been inflicted by a person of Blaise's slender physique, the prosecution speculated that after she stabbed him while he was standing, she repeatedly bludgeoned him with the aluminum baseball bat that she kept in the back seat of her car for self-protection.

Response

That speculation was unsupported by testimony. ME Simms testified that among Bailey's serious injuries (Bailey had at least 33 identifiable injuries), he suffered several bludgeoning type injuries, including "six teeth knocked out" and "skull fractures." [103] However, Simms testified Bailey "didn't have any skull fractures that were depressed like, you know, a bat would depress somebody." [104] On cross-examination he also testified that Bailey would have suffered more serious facial injuries if his teeth had been knocked out with a bat, and his skull fractures and the accompanying bleeding were consistent with his head striking a sharp edge. [105] The concrete curb next to where his body was found had a sharp edge.

Thomas Wahl, a technician with the LVMPD crime lab, also supported that Blaise's bat wasn't used to hit Bailey. He testified, "There was no blood, hairs or tissue recovered from the aluminum baseball bat or detected on that item." [106] The bat has a porous rubber handle, so even if blood had been thoroughly scrubbed off the bat's barrel with industrial strength cleaners, modern techniques would detect trace blood residue on the handle.

George Schiro, a forensic scientist of national repute, was retained by Blaise's public defenders to expertly analyze the prosecution's physical evidence. Schiro was associated with the Louisiana State Police Crime Laboratory, and with only a few exceptions he had testified on behalf of the prosecution throughout his career. His credentials were such that two years after Blaise's trial, he served in 2004 as chairperson of the national Association of Forensic DNA Analysts and Administrators. [107] Although Schiro's credentials were unassailable, he was retained only a few weeks before Blaise's trial, and that proved problematic for Judge Vega's admission of some of his testimony.

Schiro analyzed the prosecution's scenario that Bailey was knifed while standing, and then while bleeding heavily from his many wounds, he was repeatedly hit with a bat. He wrote in his Forensic Science Report: "There is no documentation of blood spatter above a height of 12 inches on any of the surrounding crime scene surfaces. ... "When a person is bleeding and repeatedly beaten with a long object, such as a baseball bat or tire iron, or is repeatedly stabbed using an arcing motion, then cast-off blood spatters corresponding to the arc of the swing are produced ...**The confined space of the crime scene enclosures and the lack of cast-off indicate**

Majority of blood splatter was less than 6" above the ground, with one splotch at about 11".

that a baseball bat was not used to beat Mr. Bailey. The beating was more likely due to a pounding or punching type motion." [108]

Thus, Bailey was not struck with a bat or other long object, but by a person's fist or something in that person's hand, like brass knuckles, or possibly a combination of the two.

Judge Vega, however, did not allow the jury to hear Schiro's exculpatory blood cast-off testimony. She sustained the prosecution's objection that Blaise's lawyers had not provided them with proper notice of the scope of his expert testimony. [109]

Schiro's analysis that Bailey was vigorously pummeled and not hit with a long object also tended to exclude Blaise for two additional reasons. He wrote in his case report:

- Even though Bailey was vigorously stabbed and beaten savagely, and "the surfaces surrounding the crime scene were abrasive and could have also caused abrasions on the killer's hands. **No cuts, abrasions, broken fingernails, or healing bruises can be seen in the photographs of Ms. Lobato's hands.**" [110]
- None of Blaise's distinctive bleach blond hairs were found among the crime scene's hairs: "During a beating and stabbing homicide, the killer can lose hair at the scene either by having it forcibly removed or through the natural hair shedding process. Bleached Caucasian hairs found at the crime scene or

associated with Bailey's body would have been significant. **There is no information indicating that any bleached blonde hairs were observed or collected from the crime scene or Mr. Bailey's body." [111]**

Vega likewise didn't allow the jury to hear Schiro's testimony about the exculpatory value of the lack of injuries to Blaise's hands and the absence of her distinctive hair at the crime scene.

In conclusion, ME Simms testimony supported that Bailey's skull fracture was consistent with his head striking concrete, indicating that Bailey fell after being shoved or punched by a physically larger and stronger person. Lab technician Wahl's testimony indicated that Blaise's bat was not used to strike any person. While forensic expert Schiro's analysis complimented Simms' and Wahl's conclusions by determining Bailey was not struck with a bat or other long object.

Seventh prosecution prong

Since Blaise described in her statement stabbing at her assailant as he hovered over her, the prosecution argued that Bailey was standing with his pants down when he was stabbed in his groin.

Response

Schiro analyzed the evidence for "vertically dripped blood": "The photographs of his pants also do not indicate the presence of any vertically dripped blood. **This indicates that he did not receive any bleeding injuries while in a standing position." [112]**

Schiro's "vertically dripped blood" analysis that Bailey didn't bleed while standing undermines the prosecution's speculation that Bailey was stabbed while standing and then beaten. His analysis also supports that Blaise was describing an entirely different incident in her statement, since she "was laying down" when she stabbed at her assailant as he hovered above her with his pants down.

Judge Vega, however, did not allow the jury to hear Schiro's exculpatory blood dripping testimony that Bailey's bleeding injuries were inflicted from him being beaten *and* stabbed while he was in a prone position. She sustained the prosecution's objection that Blaise's lawyers had not provided them with proper notice of the scope of Schiro's expert testimony.

Eighth prosecution prong

To fit Bailey's murder with Blaise's statement that she was in the midst of an intense two-week methamphetamine binge and she was continuously awake for the three days preceding being assaulted, the prosecution speculated she drove her car from Panaca to Las Vegas on July 6. They further speculated that after murdering Bailey early on the morning of July 8, Blaise went to a friend's house, got cleaned up, and then drove back to Panaca. She then parked her car on the public street in front of her parent's house to hide it.

Response

This scenario could be the narrative out of a poorly written fictional novel rejected for publication, because it is not based on facts – it is 100% speculative. Consider the following:

• The prosecution presented no evidence of any kind whatsoever, not even anything that can reasonably be considered circumstantial, that Blaise was in Las Vegas on July 6, 7 or 8. Which means *there is not any evidence* linking Blaise to Bailey's murder.

• Numerous people saw Blaise in Panaca on July 6, 7 or 8.

• People saw Blaise's car parked and unmoved in front of her parent's house.

• Phone records corroborate that Blaise's boyfriend at the time, Doug Twining, called her in Panaca from Las Vegas at least 17 times from July 2 to July 9, including several times during the late evening of July 8 and early morning of July 9, when he needed directions to her parent's house as he drove up from Las Vegas to pick her up and take her back with him.

• Blaise stated during her July 20, 2001 interrogation that she had been out of her mind on a non-stop methamphetamine binge for a week prior to, and a week after the assault against her. Bailey was killed on July 8, which means that if the attack she referred to was by Bailey, then from July 1 to 15 she would have been high on methamphetamines, going for days at a time without sleep. Yet on July 2, Blaise returned from Las Vegas to resume living at her parent's home in Panaca. None of the people who saw Blaise in and around Panaca at various times from July 2 to July 9 have testified that she was high on methamphetamines at any time. Those eyewitness accounts are consistent with the results of Blaise's blood sample taken at the Caliente Clinic on the afternoon of July 5 that didn't test positive for methamphetamines. The prosecution's speculation also dismissed that Blaise's 24-hour urine sample was collected by her mom on the morning of July 7.

• Although she was not allowed to testify about it, Blaise's mother, Becky, passed a lie detector test that included questions concerning Blaise's presence in Panaca on July 8, and specifically, that she saw Blaise sleeping on the living room futon the morning of July 8. Blaise also testified to being in Panaca on July 8, and although she wasn't allowed to tell the jury, she took and passed *three* lie detector tests that included questions concerning her presence in Panaca on July 8, the day that Duran Bailey was murdered 170 miles away in Las Vegas.

• The prosecution's argument completely ignored that Blaise also said she was out of her mind on methamphetamines for a week after she was assaulted. Doug Twining testified that after he drove from Las Vegas to Panaca on the evening of July 8 to pick her up, she stayed with him at his parent's house in Las Vegas from July 9 to July 13. He did not testify that he saw her use or exhibit any signs of methamphetamine use, and neither did anyone else.

• Dixie made no mention in her statement to Thowsen, or in her pre-trial or trial testimony, that Blaise appeared high on methamphetamines or in withdrawal during their early July conversation, and Johnson made no claim in her statement or testimony that Dixie mentioned any drug induced behavior by Blaise.

• The prosecution accepted the truthfulness of Blaise's statement that she did not have any sleep while high on methamphetamines during the three days prior to her assault, so they would logically have to accept that she was being truthful when she said at the same time that she had been out of her mind on methamphetamines during both the week before and the week after the assault.

The jury, however, was unaware of some of the alibi testimony corroborating Blaise's presence in Panaca from July 2 through July 9. (See Table 3, p. 57.) Citing inadequate notice to the prosecution, Judge Vega barred the jury from being exposed to that exculpatory information.

Defense expert Schiro's testimony limited

Vega did not allow the jury to hear the majority of defense witness Schiro's proposed expert testimony that would have undermined the prosecution's case by exposing it lacked a scientific basis. Among Schiro's findings that the jury was not allowed to hear were:

• The lack of blood cast-off on the trash enclosure's walls higher than 12″ above the ground means Bailey wasn't beaten with a bat or other long object, but that "The beating was more likely due to a pounding or punching type motion." [113]

• The uninjured condition of Blaise's hands that would be unexpected of Bailey's murderer: "No cuts, abrasions, broken fingernails, or healing bruises can be seen in the photographs of Ms. Lobato's hands." [114]

• Bailey was stabbed while lying down, and did not receive *any* bleeding injuries while standing. [115]

• Bailey's murder(s) likely left hairs at the scene, and no hairs matching Blaise's readily identifiable bleach blond hair were among those collected from the crime scene. [116]

• The bloody shoeprints leading away from Bailey's body only could have been made by the person who covered it and his blood on the ground with cardboard and trash. The only reasonable interpretation is that person was the killer, and Blaise's shoeprint is 2-1/2 to 3 sizes smaller than those bloody man's size 9 (woman's size 10-1/2) shoeprints. [117]

The jury was also not allowed to hear Schiro's crime scene reconstruction that depicts Bailey's murder as a premeditated methodically executed event. Schiro wrote in his case report:

1. The killer enters the enclosure.

2. Mr. Bailey is lying on the ground, possibly sleeping.

3. (These events cannot be sequenced. They all happened at some point, but not necessarily in the order listed. His pants could have been down prior to the stabbing or they could have come down sometime during the stabbing but prior to the scrotum wound. He might have been masturbating prior to getting killed. This could explain the presence of the adult magazines at the crime scene. He may also have fallen asleep with his pants down.) **The killer stabs the victim in the face, head, scrotum, and possibly the abdomen. At some point, Mr. Bailey's pants come down. Mr. Bailey manages to use his hands and arms in an effort to defend himself. His left carotid artery is cut while he is on the ground. Mr. Bailey is also beaten forcefully about the head with a blunt object most likely using a pounding or punching type motion or his head is slammed forcefully against the surrounding concrete.**

4. Mr. Bailey's anus was then lacerated.

5. Mr. Bailey's body was turned over.

6. The killer stabs Mr. Bailey in the abdomen and severs his penis.

7. Mr. Bailey is covered with the cardboard.

8. Trash is deposited on Mr. Bailey and the blood [on the ground].

9. The killer exits the enclosure. [118]

Schiro was allowed to testify about the testing for the presence of blood in Blaise's car. He discussed that both presumptive luminol and phenolphthalein tests were subject to a high incidence of false positives, and that negative confirmatory tests indicated to him that human blood did not cause the weakly positive presumptive tests for two spots in Blaise's car. [119]

After he had given his very limited testimony, Schiro, who had spent the overwhelming majority of his career as a prosecution witness identifying crime scene evidence that inculpated an accused person, told reporters in the courthouse hallway what Judge Vega barred him from telling Blaise's jurors: **"There is no evidence to tie Ms. Lobato to the crime scene. I feel the evidence is even exclusionary on her behalf."** [120] Schiro was even more emphatic in the conclusion to his report, "There is no evidence associating Kirstin Lobato with Duran Bailey or the crime scene. Ms. Lobato is also excluded as the source of physical evidence found at the crime scene." [121]

The prosecution's case didn't implicate Blaise in Bailey's death

At the point that the prosecution rested their case, none of their prongs substantively supported implicating Blaise as Bailey's killer. The prosecution's lack of inculpatory evidence was consistent with forensic expert Schiro's analysis of the case that Judge Vega did not allow the jury to hear.

Conclusion of Blaise's trial

The closing arguments were made on Friday, May 18, 2002. DA DiGiacomo's argument was based on a multitude of speculations about how and why it is possible that Blaise murdered Bailey.

Blaise's lawyer Kohn, emphasized that the detectives did not identify the date of the man's stabbing they were talking about when they interrogated Blaise. Furthermore, he pointed out that the detectives and prosecutors were wrongly assuming she was talking about Bailey, when none of the details of the incident she described matched those of his death. Kohn told the jury, "Two people talking about two different incidents, one coincidence that counsel has alluded to and a multitude of inconsistencies that the State chooses to ignore." [122] He compared the prosecution of Blaise to the Salem Witch Trials, during which many innocent women were put to death, "Women who were different, who were odd, who said stupid things. Who could not prove that they were not a witch, because that's what you had to do at that time, prove to me you are not a witch. Prove to me you did not do this." [123]

DA Kephart asserted in his rebuttal argument that Blaise's acknowledgment during her interrogation that she stabbed at a man's groin area to fend off his sexual assault in Las Vegas, constituted a confession to Bailey's murder.

Verdict and Sentence

Judge Vega finished reading the jury instructions at 9 p.m. The jury began deliberations immediately. [124] After five hours they announced they had arrived at a verdict. At 3 a.m. their verdicts of guilty to both counts were read in court, and Blaise, who had been free on $50,000 bond, was taken into custody.

Her lawyer Navarro told reporters, "She placed her belief in the justice system, and she ended up being convicted of a crime that she did not commit." [125]

On July 2, 2002, Blaise was sentenced to a minimum of 20 years in prison for her conviction of Bailey's first-degree murder, and a 5-year concurrent sentence for her conviction of sexual penetration of a dead human body. Judge Vega then added a 20-year sentence to be served consecutively, based on her determination that Bailey was stabbed with a knife so the deadly weapon enhancement applied. So Blaise's sentence was to serve a minimum of 40 years before becoming eligible for parole. Vega also imposed a special lifetime supervision sentence if Blaise should ever be released.

Blaise's conviction leads to efforts to publicize her case

After Blaise's conviction her family set-up a website to publicize her case. The website, Justice For Kirstin, included a time-line of Blaise's alibi of being in Panaca for the days July 6, 7 and 8. [126]

In the fall of 2003 a Las Vegas woman, Michelle Ravell, whose son had dated Blaise, spearheaded the founding of a group, Justice4Kirstin, dedicated to working towards Blaise's exoneration. They set-up a website, http://www.justice4kirstin.com that included extensive information about Blaise's case.

Justice4Kirstin contacted *Justice:Denied – the magazine for the wrongly convicted*. A year later the magazine published an article about Blaise's case in its Fall 2004 issue (Issue 26). That article, *Las Vegas Police and Prosecutors Frame Woman 170 Miles From Murder Scene - Kirstin Lobato's "Very Peculiar Story"*, was the longest feature article in the magazine's history, at more than 10,000 words. [127]

V
Blaise's Conviction Reversed And Retrial Ordered

Blaise's conviction reversed by Nevada Supreme Court on September 3, 2004

On September 3, 2004 the Nevada Supreme Court reversed Blaise's conviction and remanded her case for a new trial. *Lobato v. State*, 96 P.3d 765 (Nev. 09/03/2004). The reversal was based in part on Judge Vega's failure to allow Blaise's lawyers to cross-examine Korinda Martin about letters suggesting leniency that she wanted sent to her sentencing judge. [128] The Court noted, "The proffered letters and extrinsic evidence relating to them confirmed Martin's desperation to obtain an early release from incarceration and her willingness to adopt a fraudulent course of action to achieve that goal." [129] The Court also ruled that it was prejudicial error for Vega to bar Blaise' lawyers from calling as a witness the woman the letters were mailed to, as well as barring introduction of the letters themselves as evidence. [130] Having found sufficient grounds to reverse Blaise's conviction, the Court didn't rule on the issues of Vega's barring of exculpatory expert and alibi testimony. The Court implied any such errors could be cured during Blaise's retrial. [131]

New lawyers for Blaise's retrial

Blaise in December 2005 after her release on bail.

After reviewing her case and becoming convinced of her innocence, San Francisco based lawyers Shari Greenberger and Sara Zalkin agreed to represent Blaise *pro bono* during her retrial as co-counsel to her lead lawyer, David Schieck, with the Clark County Special Public Defenders Office. In December 2005 Blaise was released pending her retrial on a $500,000 bond posted by supporters believing in her innocence. For reasons unknown, Blaise's attorneys did not move to recuse Vega from the case in spite of her bias against Blaise suggested by her prosecution favorable errors that caused the Nevada Supreme Court to grant Blaise a new trial.

Pretrial motions favor prosecution

The Nevada Supreme Court was bluntly disappointed with the prejudicial effect of a number of Judge Vega's prosecution favorable rulings in Blaise's first trial. The pretrial motions hearings for Blaise's retrial were the first opportunity for Vega, a former Clark County, Nevada prosecutor, to indicate if she was going to continue to openly favor her former colleagues. [132] At the conclusion of those hearings in May 2006, there was no doubt she was not going to be more balanced. Vega did not grant any defense motion *in Limine* or suppression outright. The following are some of her rulings:

• The prosecution could introduce the "double hearsay" testimony of Laura Johnson about what she alleged Dixie Tienken said that Blaise said to her. The prosecution argued that Johnson would follow Tienken as a prosecution witness, and Johnson would testify about Tienken's testimony that was different than Johnson's recollection of the conversation – and her testimony would thus be admissible as a "prior inconsistent statement" by Tienken. Under the prosecution's theory, any discrepancy between Tienken's testimony and Johnson's "recollection" of their conversation on July 18, 2001, would thus be admissible under the "prior inconsistent statement" hearsay exception. There was no record of that conversation so Johnson, the prosecution's witness, would effectively be the arbiter of what was a "prior inconsistent statement" by Tienken, and thus admissible.

The defense argued that "the very basis of admitting the testimony as a "prior inconsistent statement" lacks foundation and is not substantiated by the evidence." [133] Blaise's lawyers further asserted, "By seeking to introduce this impermissible hearsay the State is trying to circumvent the rules of evidence." [134]

Judge Vega denied the defense's motion without prejudice as premature, since Johnson had not yet testified, but that the defense could object for the record when Johnson testified. Thus, Vega cleverly sided with the prosecution by allowing Johnson to give her "double hearsay" testimony without making a ruling on the motion's merits.

• The prosecution could introduce Blaise's July 20, 2001 statement, even though Blaise's lawyers argued that its details had no relevance to Bailey's death, and she advised Thowsen and LaRochelle in the statement that the incident she described occurred more than a month prior to the interrogation, and thus more than two weeks prior to Bailey's death. Blaise's lawyers also argued that before *Mirandizing* Blaise, Thowsen overborne the 18-year-old's will by psychological coercion that made her subsequent *Miranda* waiver invalid, and the statement inadmissible as "the fruit of the poisonous tree." The defense relied on *Harrison v. U.S.*, 392 U.S. 219 (1968). Judge Vega denied the motion to suppress the statement.

Blaise's lawyers overlooked the argument that Thowsen and LaRochelle drove to Lincoln County on July 20 with the purpose of arresting Blaise and seizing her car as material evidence in Bailey's murder. Regardless of whether Blaise talked to them, or whatever she may have said, she was going to be arrested for Bailey's murder. Nothing she said or didn't say was going to change the fact the detectives were going to take her back to Las Vegas as the person they believed murdered Bailey. (The fact that there is not a single detail in Blaise's statement implicating her in Bailey's murder is indicative that the detectives' purpose in traveling to Panaca was to arrest Blaise, not to investigate Bailey's murder. (See Table 1, p. 17 and Table 2, p. 19.) If she had refused to talk to the detectives she would have been immediately formally arrested. Consequently, as soon as the detectives arrived at the home of Blaise's parents she was in physical custody. Blaise would have been prevented – at gunpoint if necessary – from leaving at any time after the detectives arrived.

• The prosecution could introduce testimony about presumptive luminol tests of two spots in Blaise's car that weakly tested positive (Indicating the *possible* presence of an iron bearing substance, one of which is blood.), even though much more sophisticated and precise confirmatory tests of swabs of the two spots returned negative results for the presence of blood. [135] The prosecution's argument was that the confirmatory tests (That are 100 times more precise than the presumptive tests that commonly return a false positive for blood.) could be wrong to exclude the presence of blood – while the much *less* precise presumptive tests indicating the *possible* presence of an iron bearing substance that might *possibly* be blood could be correct. Therefore the prosecution argued the presumptive test results should be admissible as having more probative than prejudicial value.

The prosecution also argued that blood possibly could have been cleaned off the surface, thus causing the weak positive presumptive test results. That claim was contrary to the determination of Brent Turvey, an expert retained by the defense. He wrote a case report in which he noted that powerful cleaning agents available to the public, such as bleach and ammonium, cannot be expected to remove detectable traces of blood, even after repeated applications. Based on the scientific literature he wrote, "... it is most accurate to say that no blood of any kind was found in Ms. Lobato's vehicle. Furthermore, it is a reasonable scientific certainty that no blood was ever transferred to those areas in or on the car where Luminol results were negative. This precludes the possibility that the person who committed this crime also entered and operated Ms. Lobato's vehicle immediately after its commission." [136]

Blaise's lawyers argued in vain that the jury would be misled that the weakly positive presumptive tests inferred the presence of blood in Blaise's car, when they didn't in any way, because the two spots were disproven as blood by the negative confirmatory tests. Judge Vega denied the motion, ruling the probative value of the presumptive tests exceeded their prejudicial effect on the jury. Vega's ruling disregarded that the inability of the LVMPD to find any evidentiary link between Blaise's car and Bailey's murder is why Thowsen authorized its release to her dad about ten days after it was seized for inspection by the crime lab.

• The prosecution could introduce what amounted to about 140 photographs of the crime scene and Bailey's autopsy photos. Blaise's lawyers argued unsuccessfully that the cumulative effect of the photos, many that were near duplicates, would have "the principle effect of inciting and inflaming the jury, due to graphic depictions of the victim's body, the horror of the crime and the cumulative effect of unnecessarily duplicative photographs." [137] Judge Vega denied the motion, ruling the probative value of exposing the jury to the numerous and near duplicative photographs exceeded their prejudicial effect.

• The prosecution could introduce as one of the possible murder weapons, the bat found in Blaise's car when it was searched on July 20, 2001, even though it had no known connection to Bailey's murder. Scientific tests had excluded it from having any blood or biological material on its metal surface or its porous rubber handle, and ME Simms was already on record that Bailey's "blunt force" injuries, and the manner of his six teeth knocked out, were inconsistent with being caused by a bat. Vega ruled the bat's probative value as evidence exceeded its prejudicial effect on the jury.

• The prosecution could introduce pictures and testimony about Blaise's custom license plate,[138] even though her car was not found to have any connection whatsoever with Bailey's death. Her tire tracks didn't match those found at the crime scene and confirmatory scientific tests excluded the presence of any blood in her car. Vega's ruling was also inexplicable because the distinctiveness of Blaise's sporty red Fiero and its custom license plate would have made it likely that a witness to Bailey's murder or someone in the area would have remembered seeing her car. The lack of any witnesses in Las Vegas – the city that never sleeps – speaks volumes and is consistent with the numerous witnesses who say that Blaise's car, which is known to have had mechanical problems, [139] was continuously parked in Panaca from a week before Bailey's murder until it was hauled away by the police almost two weeks afterwards. Blaise's lawyers argued to no avail that the license plate had no evidentiary value, and the prosecution's sole reason for exposing the jury to a photo and testimony about it was to prejudice them against her as a "bad person" of low moral character who would commit a heinous crime. Without explanation, Vega ruled the probative value of a photo and testimony about the license plate outweighed its prejudicial effect.

Blaise's lawyers overlooked the argument that the license plate's absence of evidentiary value is underscored by the fact that the prosecution had to introduce a photo of it, because Thowsen didn't consider it important enough to seize from Blaise's car before he authorized her dad to retrieve it from the LVMPD impound yard.

• Judge Vega denied the defense's motion to dismiss the charges based on "the state's failure to preserve and collect exculpatory evidence." That evidence included Bailey's penis that even though it was handled by his killer, was not collected as evidence, but instead was put in a manila envelope and transported with his body when it was taken to the medical examiner's office for autopsy. Bailey's penis was then buried with his body. That evidence also included white paper towels "stuffed in the open wound" in Bailey's genital area that were likewise presumably handled by Bailey's killer, and which were not collected as evidence but discarded. Also, three cigarette butts found on Bailey's body under the plastic in which he was wrapped, were not examined for latent prints or the presence of identifiable DNA. Blaise's lawyers argued the failure to collect and/or preserve the potentially exculpatory crime scene evidence for testing was a fatal due process violation caused by the "bad faith," or at a minimum the "gross negligence" of the police.

The prosecution countered by claiming that because Bailey's killer (or killers) was unknown at the time the crime scene evidence was collected, the investigators didn't know what items to discard or collect for testing in order to identify the killer or killers. Prosecutor DiGiacomo argued, "... at the time that they processed the scene, they had no idea who their suspect was going to be." [140] Blaise's lawyers responded that identifying Bailey's unknown assailant(s) was why collecting and testing the crime scene evidence was a critical police responsibility.

Judge Vega denied the motion on the basis that Blaise's lawyers hadn't proven the uncollected and/or untested evidence was in fact exculpatory. She also said that in July 2001 the crime scene investigators and police could not have been expected to know that fingerprints and scientific testing, such as DNA, could possibly identify Bailey's murderer(s) from their handling of any particular item. Therefore, the police and investigators couldn't have acted in "bad faith" in failing to collect and preserve the crime scene evidence. Vega's assertion is contrary to the use of DNA testing and fingerprints to identify criminal suspects beginning in 1986 and 1910, respectively. [141] Also contrary to Vega's assertion, both techniques of suspect identification were commonly known to law enforcement personal for many years prior to Bailey's murder. Further undermining the basis for Vega's ruling is that the hit television series *CSI: Crime Scene Investigations*, is set in Las Vegas. The program's first season was 2000, and it routinely portrays sophisticated forensic examination techniques, including DNA and fingerprints, as useful to Las Vegas police investigators in the identification of a crime's suspect. [142]

Months after the motion was denied, and after Blaise's retrial began in September 2006, DiGiacomo secretly ordered the LV Metro PD Crime Lab to test the three cigarette butts mentioned in the motion to dismiss. The test results were disclosed to the defense during the trial's second week. One butt had no isolatable DNA, the second had DNA from Bailey's blood and an unidentified person who was not Blaise, and the third butt not only excluded Blaise, but had the DNA profile of an unidentified male. So the weakness of Judge Vega's "rationale" in denying the motion to dismiss was exposed when two of the cigarette butts that were untested at the time of the defense's motion, proved to be exculpatory evidence for Blaise.

• Judge Vega also denied a defense motion to dismiss the charges on the basis that the prosecution "cannot establish the *corpus delicti* of the crime with evidence independent of defendant's extrajudicial admissions." [143] Just weeks before the motion was heard, the Nevada Supreme Court reiterated, "It has long been black letter law in Nevada that the *corpus delicti* of a crime must be proven independently of the defendant's extra-judicial admissions." *Edwards v. State*, 132 P.3d 581 (Nev. 04/27/2006). Even though the defendant's lawyers did not raise the "corpus delicti" issue in his appeal, the Court in *Edwards* decided *sua sponte*, "...we conclude that his conviction based solely upon his extra-judicial admission constitutes plain, clear error affecting his substantial rights. As such, the error warrants reversal on this separate and independent ground." *Id*.

Due to the absence of any evidence independent of her July 20, 2001, statement and her other purported extra-judicial statements, Blaise's lawyers argued that contrary to the prohibition by the Nevada Supreme Court, the prosecution relied solely on her extra-judicial statements "to prove the corpus delicti of Bailey's homicide." [144] Although Vega was aware that there must be independent evidence of Blaise's guilt apart from interpretations and recollections of her purported extra-judicial statements, she nevertheless denied the motion. [145]

• Judge Vega did backhandedly grant one motion. The defense's moved to have the May 2002 testimony of defense witness Diann Parker, who had died, read into the record. Then, in response to the prosecution oral request during the hearing, Vega ruled that Parker's testimony would be read during the prosecution's case. Blaise's lawyers argued to no avail that reading Parker's testimony during the prosecution's case would create the false impression to the jury that she was a prosecution witness, when she was actually a defense witness.

Although the prosecution did not cite a single legal authority in opposing several of the defense motions that were based on extensive legal authorities, and some of those prosecution responses were barely a page in length, Judge Vega, a former Clark County DA, overwhelmingly sided with the Clark County DA's Office during the motion's hearings. Thus it was evident from Vega's pretrial rulings that she was going to allow the prosecutors free-reign to run a replay of Blaise's first trial.

Pubic hair DNA tests excluded Blaise in September 2006

Several weeks before Blaise's retrial was scheduled to begin on September 11, 2006, the prosecution disclosed that it had ordered DNA testing of a pubic hair found during a combing of Bailey's pubic hair on the day his body was discovered. The hair that had remained untested for more than five years in Bailey's rape kit, even though the defense had repeatedly asked for it to be tested.

The DNA test excluded Blaise and Bailey as the hair's source, but it did reveal that it came from an unidentified male. That finding, more than five years after Bailey's murder, was consistent with ME Simms' testimony during Blaise's May 2002 trial that the manner of Bailey's murder had homosexual overtones.

Retrial begins September 11, 2006

Judge Vega allotted three weeks for the retrial based on the representation of the prosecution and the defense on how long their respective cases would take. Thus when jury selection began on Monday, September 11, 2006, the jury was expected to be deliberating by Friday, September 29.

Prosecution surprise – No Korinda Martin testimony during retrial

The prosecution had let it be known during pretrial proceedings that they intended to present the same case during Blaise's retrial as during her first trial. That, however, wasn't true. The defense found out during opening statements that Korinda Martin wouldn't be called as a prosecution witness. The prosecution may have been influenced to omit Martin as a witness because the defense contended in a pretrial motion to exclude Martin's testimony that allowing her testimony would constitute subornation of perjury by prosecutors DiGiacomo and Kephart. [146] The prosecutors also knew, unlike Blaise's first trial, that based on Vega's pretrial rulings they didn't need Martin's testimony.

Prosecution's strategy: "It is possible Blaise did it."

Since there was no physical, forensic, scientific, circumstantial, eyewitness or confession evidence linking Blaise, her car, or any item of hers to have been within 170 miles of Las Vegas at the time of Bailey's murder, the prosecution's primary tactic was: In spite of the lack of evidence, "It is possible she did it." The defense had timely filed its notice of an alibi defense, and over a dozen witnesses were scheduled to testify who would place Blaise in Panaca from July 2 to 9. So the success of the prosecution's "It is possible" strategy depended in part on their success at blocking anyone from testifying about their knowledge of the attack on Blaise six weeks before Bailey's murder.

Medical examiner Simms testifies

ME Simms testified to the extent of Bailey's wounds. He said that in a career encompassing 4,500 to 4,600 autopsies he had encountered a number of cases in which a man (or men) had severed a dead man's penis, but none of the cases involved a woman. [147] He also testified he had never read in professional literature of a case involving a woman's sexual dismemberment of a dead man. Simms further testified that it was a "sexually motivated homicide," [148] and that the manner of Bailey's death suggested it involved a homosexual encounter. [149] He also testified that it was within the realm of possibility that Bailey could have died anywhere from 8-24 hours prior to the time the coroners investigator pronounced him dead at 3:50 a.m., [150] but to a "medical certainty" he died 12-18 hours before pronouncement of death, or between 9:50 a.m. and 3:50 p.m. [151]

Simms also testified that Bailey's "blunt force trauma" wounds were inconsistent with being caused by a bat, because they didn't have the indentation a bats curved surface would leave on the skulls soft tissue, and there were cracks in Bailey's skull consistent with it being struck or him striking a surface with a sharp edge. [152] Bailey's body was found lying next to a sharp-edged concrete curb, but no object identifiable as the cause of his trauma injuries was found during the investigation of Bailey's murder. He also testified it was unlikely a bat was used to knock out Bailey's teeth, because there wasn't the accompanying type of facial and jaw bone damage a bat blow would cause. [153] In spite of its improbability, Kephart did get Simms to testify that it was "possible" some of Bailey's injuries could have been caused by a bat.

Simms further testified that some of Bailey's wounds were so deep that they were likely inflicted by an object with at least a 6″ cutting edge. [154] Thowsen's subsequent testimony and Blaise's statement established that her butterfly knife had a 3-1/2″ to 4″ blade.

LVMPD crime lab technician Thomas Wahl testifies

Thomas Wahl was the LVMPD crime lab technician who performed many of the forensic tests conducted in July and August 2001 on evidence recovered from Bailey's crime scene, and on Blaise's car and personal items. He testified about his findings, the long and short of which was that none of the crime scene evidence was identifiable as originating from Blaise, and none of Bailey's blood or DNA was identifiable as being on any of Blaise's personal items or in her car. In regard to that evidence Wahl's testimony mirrored what he told the jury during Blaise first trial.

Wahl did, however, provide new testimony concerning "the swabbings of the penis of Duran Bailey and swabbings of the rectal or rectum of Duran Bailey at the time of autopsy to determine if any evidence of semen was present." [155] In preparation for Blaise's retrial, the prosecution contracted with a private forensic laboratory, Myriad Genetic Laboratories, to examine evidence in Bailey's rape kit. The rape kit evidence included Bailey's rectal and penis swabbings. Myriad issued a report of its findings dated February 13, 2006. On direct examination Wahl read from the reports Results and Conclusions: "Semen was detected on Items 1B," which were penile swabs, "and Item 2A," rectal swabs." [156] The following exchange then took place between Kephart and Wahl:

> ### New scientific techniques can obtain DNA profile from semen lacking sperm
>
> Five months after Blaise's 2006 trial, *New Scientist* magazine reported in its March 7, 2007 issue that a new scientific testing technique developed in England was first used in a January 2007 rape case to detect a full male DNA profile from spermless semen intermixed with a female's DNA. In October 2007 Bode Technology performed its first commercial tests using a DNA technique that can isolate and identify a DNA profile from a male's spermless semen intermixed with the DNA of another male. Proof that Bailey's murderer was a man could be ascertained with this new technique, if the sperm-free semen on Bailey's rectal swabs could be matched to the DNA profile identified on the crime scene chewing gum or cigarette butts. The new techniques also place new importance on DNA testing Bailey's penis, since the DNA profile of the person who handled it, and of the person whose semen is on it, may now be isolated from Bailey's DNA.
>
> See, Rapists snared by sperm-free semen, *New Scientist*, March 7, 2007, p. 16.

By Mr. Kephart:

Q. "Okay. Did it go further as to identifying whose semen it is?"

A. Well, in order to do a DNA analysis, the next step would be to determine if any sperm cells were identified on the smears that are prepared by the medical examiner from the swabs. ... And so Myriad, it appears that they had examined the slides made from the penile swabs and the rectal swabs and the oral swabs. ...

...

Q. Okay. Were they able to determine the source of the semen.

A. They then examined the penile smears and the rectal smears and they did not identify sperm, so they went no further. There was no sperm to identify. There's no sperm cells to get a DNA profile from so they didn't proceed any further at that point. [157]

On cross-examination Schieck did not raise the issue of the semen recovered from Bailey's rectum. He did, however, mention the swabs during his closing argument, but only in regards to the pubic hair in the rape kit recovered from Bailey's body that Myriad Labs didn't DNA test because of the cost of doing so. (That pubic hair was tested by the LVMPD crime lab just prior to the start of Blaise's retrial, and Blaise and Bailey were excluded as the source.)

Dixie Tienken testifies

Dixie had been Blaise's adult education teacher when she earned her GED at 17. Blaise considered Dixie her friend and during a three hour conversation in early July 2001 that covered many topics, Blaise mentioned she had fended off a sexual assault with her knife when she had been staying in Las Vegas. [158] Dixie didn't provide any testimony specifically linking Blaise to Bailey's murder, and she actually provided testimony supporting that the attack Blaise described had occurred between one and two months prior to their conversation. However, Dixie's testimony was necessary for the prosecution to lay the foundation for their "star witness" Laura Johnson's double hearsay testimony about what Johnson claimed Dixie told her Blaise had said.

Since Dixie's testimony as a prosecution witness was primarily important to the degree that it differed from Johnson's expected testimony, prosecutor DiGiacomo's strategy was to undermine Dixie's credibility by trying to paint her as not just Blaise's former teacher, but as an adult friend who would protect Blaise by coloring her testimony. To create the impression that Dixie was an unreliable witness, DiGiacomo baited and prodded at her while treating her like an adversary. After being unable to shake Dixie's composure and testimony that didn't implicate Blaise in Bailey's murder, DiGiacomo successfully motioned Judge Vega to declare Dixie a "hostile witness." Even with DiGiacomo's gloves off and all her pretenses of civility out the window, Dixie didn't waver in her testimony, in spite of being pounded on with DiGiacomo's "bare knuckles" verbal assault.

"Star Witness" Laura Johnson testifies

During Laura Johnson subsequent "double hearsay" testimony, she testified that Dixie said Blaise said that when she was coming out of a strip club where she worked in Las Vegas, a man attacked her while his penis was hanging out of his pants and she cut it off. Johnson also said Dixie said that Blaise said she was "hiding out" at her parents house and her parents were trying to get rid of her car, or get it painted to hide it. Thus Johnson provided the magic phrases suggesting Blaise had a "guilty mind," which Dixie denied during her testimony being told by Blaise, and which Dixie also denied telling Johnson. [159] First, that Blaise had been "hiding out" in Panaca, and second, that she wanted to "get rid" of her car or "hide" it by painting it. As a law enforcement officer expressing certainty of what Dixie told her, the prosecution would expect the jury to believe what she said over what Dixie, a teacher and Blaise's friend, said.

The prosecution didn't corroborate Johnson's testimony by presenting testimonial (auto paint shop employee or person told by the Lobato's about any car painting or disposal plans) or documentary evidence (a newspaper ad to sell the car or a car painting estimate) – because no such evidence exists. In fact, Blaise's bright red Fiero was parked in plain view on the public street in front of the Lobato's house until it was seized by the LVMPD and transported to Las Vegas.

The defense objected to Johnson's hearsay testimony, but Vega admitted it under the "prior inconsistent statements" hearsay exception, to the degree that it differed from Tienken's testimony about their conversation on July 18, 2001.

The irony of Johnson's testimony that made her a "star" prosecution witness, is that not only were key points contradicted by Dixie and independently uncorroborated, but her statement to the detectives about what Dixie supposedly told her shows she may have a "bathtub memory." Johnson couldn't even accurately remember some details she had told detective Thowsen on the telephone only a few hours before she gave her statement when he drove up to Lincoln County on the afternoon of July 20. Consequently, Dixie's recollection is as likely as not the accurate version of the conversation between her and Johnson. However, during their cross-examination of Johnson Blaise's lawyers didn't question the accuracy of her memory, so it wasn't brought to the jury's attention.

Detective Thowsen testifies

During Detective Thowsen's direct testimony and cross-examination, he described informally visiting Diann Parker on July 9 after being told she had been at Bailey's murder scene asking about Bailey. Thowsen also described her telling him that Bailey beat and raped her on July 1 after several Mexican's in her apartment complex told him earlier that day to leave her alone after he slapped and threatened her while she was drinking beer with them. Thowsen then talked to the apartment manager, who in providing him with the names used by the Mexicans said they didn't cause any trouble. After Thowsen ran a background check on the names that returned nothing, he didn't make any effort to question the Mexicans.

Although Bailey's murder was rich with fertile leads, including that he died with cocaine and alcohol in his system (Who were his sources of drugs and where did he hang out drinking?), his death was considered by the medical examiner to be homosexually related (Who were his homosexual partners and where did he meet them?), the manner of his death suggested revenge was the motive (Who had he crossed or otherwise given reason to seek retribution?), he lived in the trash enclosure (Who did he spend time with in the area?), and he had a violent streak (Who besides Parker had he harmed?), Thowsen did no more "investigating" into Bailey's case until getting a call from Johnson on July 20 about her conversation with Dixie. He testified to doing a background check on Blaise, and contacting the Lincoln County Sheriff's Office that he would be driving up that afternoon with another detective and a crime scene analyst to arrest a murderess.

Since Thowsen made the initial decision to arrest Blaise based on Johnson's phone call, nothing Blaise said, or even if she hadn't given a statement, would have affected her arrest. Even if Blaise had invoked her right to remain silent and said nothing she would have been formally arrested for Bailey's murder and taken back to Las Vegas. Thowsen was so hell-bent on arresting Blaise on July 20 that it wasn't until six days later, and three days after she was charged with murder, that he and LaRochelle interviewed Dixie, the source of Johnson's third-hand information the detective's relied on to arrest and charge Blaise.

> Thowsen didn't interview Dixie Tienken until six days after he arrested Blaise based on Laura Johnson's third-hand information about what she said Dixie told her that Blaise had said about a sexual assault in Las Vegas.

Thowsen testified that sometime after Blaise's arrest he went to the Budget Suites where Blaise said she had been assaulted, but he was vague as to what he did there insofar as investigating the events described in her statement. He testified that he didn't know when he went to the Budget Suites, who he talked with, that he didn't take LaRochelle or a crime scene investigator to take photographs or impound evidence, and he did not take any notes, write a report, or have any record of any kind substantiating that he had ever been at the Budget Suites as a part of investigating Bailey's homicide.

During defense attorney David Schieck's cross-examination, Thowsen was asked why he didn't thoroughly investigate the Budget Suites attack that Blaise described in her statement before arresting her, Thowsen replied, "there's no sense looking for a witness to something that we know didn't happen there." [160] Thowsen elaborated that every detail in Blaise's statement that is inconsistent with Bailey's crime scene or manner of death is explainable as "minimizing." Which he described as a guilty person's technique of lying about what he or she did to reduce its seriousness.

Thowsen's testimony about Blaise's alleged "minimizing" was critical to the prosecution, because nothing in her statement identified her as involved in Bailey's murder. (See Table 1, p. 17 and Table 2, p. 19.) Thus Thowsen had to explain away the complete absence of incriminating information in Blaise's statement. What Schieck didn't know during his cross-examination was that Thowsen fabricated his explanation that there were no identifiable details in Blaise's statement linking her to Bailey's murder because she had "minimized" her involvement.

According to the FBI and other experts in police interrogation techniques, "minimizing" is what a *detective* does to induce a suspect who has already admitted to an identifiable level of involvement in a crime to further incriminate him or herself by confessing to more specific details. The following are excerpts from an article in the August 2005 issue of the *FBI Law Enforcement Bulletin*, titled, "Reducing a Guilty Suspect's Resistance to Confessing":

Did Thowsen go to the Budget Suites Hotel?

When this author went to the Budget Suites Hotel (4855 E Boulder Hwy.) on the morning of September 28, 2006, I questioned a maintenance person, I asked questions of front desk personnel (and obtained a business card and brochure for the motel), and I asked questions of the manager as we walked around the area of the motel fronting on Boulder Highway (and I obtained his business card). I also took twenty photographs and did additional walking around the motel property and verified the layout described in Blaise's statement (fountain, stores across the street, Sam's Town casino, etc.). I also made a phone call and left a voice message that included a mention that I was at the Budget Suites, and I received a bus fair receipt for the trip from my downtown hotel. Thus as a natural part of going to the Budget Suites to investigate Blaise's statement, my presence there can independently be corroborated in at least six ways: The multiple witnesses I talked with, my possession of Budget Suites business cards and a brochure, notes and drawings I made, the photographs I took, telephone records, and a bus receipt. As a natural consequence of seeking to learn information about Blaise's statement I left a trail a mile wide that I had been at the Budget Suites. Yet Thowsen admitted that as a detective on official business during a homicide investigation he left no trail whatsoever that he had been to the Budget Suites. It is left for the reader to assess Thowsen's honesty as to whether he testified truthfully when he said he went to the Budget Suites during his investigation of Bailey's murder after Blaise's arrest. Another thing to consider is that if Thowsen did not go to the Budget Suites, what other aspects of his testimony was he not truthful about in order to aid the prosecution and/or to create the appearance that he performed as a professional detective while investigating the murder of Duran Bailey?

An interrogation is a critical component in nearly every criminal investigation. Obtaining a confession during an interrogation increases the likelihood of a conviction in court and, in many cases, is the only means to successfully resolving an investigation in the absence of other evidence. Investigators initially must control and direct the conversation during interrogations. ...

The investigator presents the acceptable reasons to confess, usually in one of three nonexclusive and nonexhaustive categories: rationalizations, projections of blame, and *minimizations*. ... Finally, investigators can try to reduce, or *minimize*, the heinous nature of the crime so it produces less guilt or shame for the suspect. The themes do not provide legal excuses for the crimes but, rather, moral and ethical justifications. Suspects will reduce their initial resistance to concealing the truth if they accept the justifications. ...

...

Because the focus of the rational choice theory is centered on self-interest, projecting the blame on anything else is appropriate to reduce the suspect's feelings of guilt. ... The investigator might blame the boyfriend for not giving the offender a chance to reconcile the relationship or for treating her poorly during the separation. Finally, the investigator can *minimize* the woman's shame by acknowledging her righteousness in deciding to stop committing criminal acts before the situation became out of control. The investigator should suggest that her choice to refrain from further acts of vandalism or even violence makes the incident rather mundane and insignificant.

...

To make the crime more acceptable, the investigator can *minimize* the suspect's deviant actions by explaining how he has seemingly overcome overwhelming natural circumstances and, despite having the uncontrollable propensity to commit more crimes, he has show considerable restraint.

...

Regarding *minimizations*, the investigators could suggest that engaging in property crimes to obtain the American dream offers a much more acceptable route than committing violent crimes.

...

The investigator can project blame on the existence of original sin or the actions of Adam and Eve for initiating the deviant act. To *minimize* the crime, the investigator can convince the suspect that his actions were minor offenses ... in comparison with the egregious acts committed by others directed at defying God (e.g., explaining that the suspect's theft from his employer pales in comparison with other cases the investigator worked where subjects stole from churches and schools). [161]

The preceding explanation of "minimization" in an official FBI publication clarifies that during Blaise's interrogation neither Thowsen or LaRochelle "minimized" any purported involvement by her in Bailey's murder. Further undermining the credibility of Thowsen's testimony about "minimization" is that Blaise said *nothing* to reduce her involvement in the attack that she described in her statement. Furthermore, her recorded statement shows that she openly and plainly stated what happened when she was assaulted, and she forthrightly answered questions by Thowsen and LaRochelle.

That the absence of incriminating information in Blaise's statement about Bailey's murder was due to her truthfulness is enhanced by the following facts: Blaise was eighteen; she had grown-up in a small town of 761 people (2000) in a large (10,634 sq. mi.) isolated county of 4,165 people (2000); [162] she had not been in legal trouble and had never been arrested, so she wouldn't have known from experience to "game" the system by downplaying involvement in a crime; and anyone who listens to her taped statement is well aware that she was in a highly emotional state of mind and talking in a free flowing steam of consciousness manner that wasn't calculating in any way.

Also undermining Thowsen's assertion that Blaise wasn't truthful in her statement, is that Dixie's July 26, 2001 statement to Thowsen of what Blaise told her in confidence doesn't deviate in significant detail from Blaise's statement. Dixie actually reinforces key exclusionary points in Blaise's statement, including that the attack occurred when it was dark and immediately afterward she left her car at Jeremy Davis' house. [163] Davis testified that Blaise parked her car at his house (on May 23, 24, or 25) just before the Memorial Day weekend. [164]

Thowsen's testimony about "minimizing" to explain away the absence of similarity between Blaise's statement and the details of Bailey's death wasn't a minor infraction. It was a cornerstone of his testimony – and of the prosecution's case against Blaise. [165] Defense attorney Schieck could have severely undermined Thowsen's testimony about "minimizing" if he had known that it lacked foundation.

The truthfulness of Thowsen's testimony was also suspect concerning his alleged effort to check-out Blaise's statement by attempting to find out if a groin area knife wound was treated by a Las Vegas medical facility. Nevada law requires that healthcare providers report non-accident related knife wounds to a "law enforcement agency." (NRS 629.041) Thowsen testified that on a day he couldn't specify his secretary allegedly telephoned medical facilities that he couldn't specify, to find out if they had treated a slashed or severed penis during May, June and July of 2001. The defense made a motion to strike Thowsen's hearsay testimony, but Judge Vega denied it based on the curious rationale that because the defense exposed on cross-examination that Thowsen's testimony was hearsay, they could not object to it. Thowsen also testified that on days he couldn't specify that he made several phone calls to persons he couldn't specify in an effort to find out if a stab wound to a man's groin had been treated. Just as with his alleged visit to the Budget Suites Hotel, Thowsen testified he made no notes of anything his secretary or anyone he called told him, he wrote no reports about the alleged medical records contacts, and he received nothing in writing from his secretary or any person or organization that was allegedly contacted by either him or his secretary. [166]

Prosecution's case lacked evidence implicating Blaise

There were several dozen witnesses during the prosecution's nearly three-week case. Those witnesses included police officers, several crime lab technicians, medical examiner's office personnel, relatives of Bailey, and friends and acquaintances of Blaise. What is notable about those witnesses is that not a single one provided any testimony linking Blaise to any involvement in Bailey's murder, or that on July 8 she had been within 170 miles of Las Vegas, or that she had ever met Bailey, or that prior to his murder she had ever been to the location of his death. Not even the two key witnesses, Johnson, who only had "double hearsay" testimony to offer, and Thowsen, whose testimony was based in part on a misleading characterization of "minimization," provided testimony that was anything more than conjecture that Blaise possibly could have been referring to Bailey's death when she described fending off a sexual assault with her knife.

That lack of testimonial evidence was backed up by the absence of any physical, forensic or scientific evidence that Blaise or her car was present at the crime scene. Her involvement was in fact undermined by the crime scene fingerprints that excluded her; the DNA test of the pubic hair found on Bailey's body excluded her; the bloody male shoeprints that excluded her; the tire tracks that excluded her car; the DNA on chewing gum found on the cardboard covering Bailey's body that excluded her; and the DNA on two cigarette butts found on Bailey's body, and underneath the plastic sheeting cover it, that excluded her. (The DNA on one butt was specifically identified as from a male.)

During cross-examination of law enforcement witnesses the defense was repeatedly able to expose the multiple deficiencies in the collection, preservation, and/or testing of crime scene evidence. Many dozens (if not over a hundred) items handled by Bailey's killer(s) were discarded at the scene. Other items collected in evidence bags were later discarded without being logged in as evidence. A number of items collected and retained as evidence and that were likely to have either been handled by the killer(s) or that could otherwise identify them, were not tested by the LVMPD Crime Lab. The portrait painted by the defense's cross-examination was that with a few exceptions, the LVMPD handled Bailey's crime scene and investigation like they were a cross between the Keystone Cops and rank amateurs. Given the inept handling of Blaise's case, it is somewhat ironic that the hit television series about crack crime scene investigators, *CSI: Crime Scene Investigations*, is set in Las Vegas. [167]

Based on their pretrial representation to Judge Vega the prosecution was scheduled to rest its case on Thursday, September 21. However, the prosecution consumed a lot of time in presenting its case that didn't involve introducing evidence linking Blaise to Bailey's murder. The days dragged on as Kephart and DiGiacomo had witness after witness identify picture after picture of the crime scene, Bailey's penis, and his autopsy photos, and testify to other inane details. At the end of the day on the 21st the prosecution wasn't close to resting. So they continued as the clock was ticking closer to the scheduled end of the trial on September 29.

The defense expressed concerns to Judge Vega on and off the record that the prosecution's slow pace was cutting into the time allotted to the defense, but she didn't seem concerned. A sore point with the defense was that on Friday, September 22, Vega recessed the trial for the weekend at 11:45 a.m. (after only 1-1/2 hours of court) to accommodate DiGiacomo's attendance that weekend at an out-of-state social event (a wedding). Finally, just prior to noon on September 29, the prosecution rested its case in chief. By that time Vega had grudgingly recognized that the defense had timely filed its notice of alibi defense and the testimony of two experts, so she knew she couldn't forestall the defense from presenting its case without being slapped down on appeal in the event of Blaise's conviction. Some of the jurors, however, were visibly disappointed when informed the trial would be continuing into the following week.

Two defense experts

The defense did not retain Schiro for Blaise's retrial, but it did enlist two experts who testified: medical doctor Michael Laufer, and forensic scientist and criminal profiler Brent Turvey. [168]

Dr. Michael Laufer testifies Bailey was likely murdered with scissors

Dr. Michael Laufer is associated with Stanford Medical School and he is a nationally recognized inventor of more than 100 medically related products. [169] Laufer had worked with Shari Greenberger on a previous case, and he agreed to provide his expertise *pro bono*.

In the course of reviewing the autopsy report, and autopsy and crime scene photos, Laufer began doubting that Bailey's stab and slashing wounds were caused by a knife, as he had been told when he agreed to review the case. He noticed they resembled scissors wounds he had treated during his years as an emergency room doctor. So he proceeded to conduct a photographed controlled experiment to see if he could duplicate Bailey's wounds by stabbing scissors into a flesh substitute – foam rubber tightly covered with ultra suede.

In his final report, dated September 24, 2006, Laufer determined that Bailey's stab wounds were consistent with being caused by scissors, and that barber scissors with a finger hook were the most likely type used to inflict Bailey's wounds. He also concluded that scissors were likely used to snip Bailey's carotid artery, and

"The penile amputation was most likely performed with scissors. Evidence exists suggesting that the penis was pulled upward while the decedent was supine." [170]

Laufer's experiment that duplicated a wound to Bailey's abdomen disclosed "a "ring distance" between the inside of the second finger and the inside of the fifth finger of the assailant's hand of at least 5.8 cm." [171] The "ring distance" of Blaise's hand was measured to be 4.3 cm. Thus Laufer concluded her hand is much smaller than the hand of Bailey's assailant. Although Laufer didn't include it in his report, since the assailant's hand is 35% larger than Blaise's hand, he is likely a male. That conclusion is consistent with all the crime scene evidence that is exclusively identifiable as originating from males.

Laufer also determined that because the bleeding of Bailey's blood stopped at the waist level of his pants, the wounds above his waist were inflicted while his pants were pulled up. He also expressed the opinion that what looked liked slicing in Bailey's anal area could have been caused by the seam of his pants when he was kicked by his scissors wielding assailant(s). [172] Which means that wound occurred before his pants were pulled down and his penis amputated. [173]

Laufer testified to his findings about Bailey's wounds and cause of death on direct examination. The prosecution, however, successfully blocked his testimony about the case's extensive blood evidence. Judge Vega agreed with the prosecutor's objection that the defense had not provided the required notice about the extent of Laufer's expert testimony.

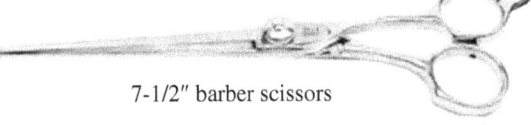

7-1/2" barber scissors

Kephart attempted during his cross-examination of Laufer to discredit his findings by suggesting it was a novel idea of an imaginative inventor to conclude Bailey's wounds were caused by scissors. Laufer responded that scissors are a common cause of stabbing and slicing wounds, and scissors caused wounds are regularly treated in emergency rooms. Kephart was taken aback during his cross-examination when Laufer testified that he provided his expertise in Blaise's case *pro bono*. Laufer said, "The first thing I was told [by defense lawyer Greenberger] was, "We don't have any money.""

butterfly knife with 3-1/2" blade
(This butterfly knife has the same blade length as Blaise's knife, but it is not an exact replica of her knife.)

Brent Turvey testifies there is no physical evidence implicating Blaise in Bailey's murder

The other defense expert was Brent Turvey, a forensic scientist and criminal profiler. After analyzing a large number of case reports and documents, Turvey completed a report dated October 17, 2005. His findings were:

1. There is no physical evidence associating Kirstin "Blaise" Lobato, or her vehicle (a red 1984 Fiero), to the crime scene.
2. The offender in this case would have transferred bloodstains to specific areas of any vehicle they entered and operated.
3. The failure of Luminol to luminesce at any of the requisite sites in the defendant's vehicle is a reasonably certain indication that blood was not ever present, despite any conventional attempts at cleaning.
4. There are several items of potentially exculpatory evidence that were present on or with the body at the crime scene but subsequently not submitted to the crime lab for analysis.
5. A primary motive in this case is directed anger expressed in the form of brutal injury, overkill and sexual punishment to the victim's genitals.
6. The wound patterns in this case may be used to support a theory of multiple assailants. [174]

Turvey also wrote in his report:

A nationwide *Westlaw* search of state and federal appellate cases revealed only 16 homicides where an adult victim's penis was actually cut off. In all but one case it was a male, or a group of two or more males, who committed the murder and the ultimate removal of the victim's penis:

• Most of the cases involved brutal attacks to the victim prior to death, even torture in some cases, and evidence of overkill.
• 7 of the cases involved multiple male offenders (2-8).
• More than 1/3 of the cases involved homosexual offenders.
• Notably, the alleged circumstances in only one case involved a female acting alone to attack, subdue, and remove the penis of an adult male victim – *Nevada v. Kirstin Blaise Lobato.* [175]

Turvey testified to his findings on direct examination. Key points of his testimony revolved around the "scientific method," and that forensic science's "exchange principle is that every contact leaves a trace." [176] He further testified that principle means a forensic scientist must have "humility before the evidence," and that "if you have no evidence, then you have no proof of contact." [177] The "exchange principle" was the basis of Turvey's conclusion that there is no physical evidence Blaise was involved in his murder, since there was no evidence at the crime scene, in her car, or on any item in her possession linking her to the scene of Bailey's murder.

Turvey's cross-examination was much more contentious than Laufer's, since it was conducted by DiGiacomo, who has a manner more unrefined and abrasive than Kephart. The biggest fireworks occurred when Turvey resisted DiGiacomo's attempts to induce him to acknowledge that the two spots in Blaise's car that weakly tested positive after a presumptive test, "possibly" could be blood. [178] Turvey repeatedly responded that the much more precise confirmatory testing of the spots were negative for blood, so the idea it was blood "had to be let go." They also had a spirited exchange when DiGiacomo repeatedly tried to get Turvey to acknowledge that the bloody male shoeprints leading away from Bailey's body "possibly" were made by a man other than his killer. Turvey said several times that he would be embarrassed as a professional to suggest the shoeprints were made by anyone other than a man involved in Bailey's murder.

Turvey also raised the ire of DiGiacomo when he responded to one of her questions by saying the prosecution should have evidence of a defendant's guilt when seeking a conviction that will result in a sentence of life in prison.

An interesting aspect of DiGiacomo's cross-examination of Turvey is Judge Vega didn't enforce the rule against asking questions that have already been answered. In spite of defense objections, Vega repeatedly allowed DiGiacomo to belligerently ask forms of the same question over and over in an effort to get Turvey to change his opinion that some piece of the prosecution's physical "evidence" didn't implicate Blaise in Bailey's murder. One courtroom spectator described DiGiacomo's unrestrained verbal bludgeoning of Turvey over and over as "painful to watch."

Turvey did seem to catch DiGiacomo off-guard once. That was during his criticism of the unprofessional handling of the investigation at Bailey's murder scene. He responded to one of her questions by saying that each and every item covering Bailey's body should have been collected, and cataloged, and tested as evidence. He explained that Bailey's killer(s) handled each of those items, and based on the "exchange principle" that every contact leaves a trace, any one of the many discarded evidentiary items could have yielded information identifying his killer(s).

Three witnesses not allowed to testify about attack on Blaise before Bailey's death

The prosecution knew that prior to Bailey's murder Blaise talked with at least six people about the May 2001 Budget Suites assault. Those six people are Stephen (Steve) Pyszkowski, Kathy Renninger, Michelle Austria, Heather McBride, Blaise's dad Larry Lobato, and a woman known as Mumblina. During Blaise's first trial Vega had allowed Pyszkowski, Austria and McBride to testify that they were told about the assault against Blaise in Las Vegas on days that ranged from a month to six days preceding Bailey's murder on July 8. [179] Larry was told by Blaise about the attack in late June 2001, but he wasn't called as a witness by the defense in Blaise's first trial.

Four of those people, Pyszkowski, Austria, McBride, and Larry Lobato testified at Blaise's retrial. However, by sustaining the prosecution's objections it was hearsay, Judge Vega blocked defense witnesses McBride and Larry Lobato from testifying about their complete knowledge of the Las Vegas assault, and Pyszkowski wasn't allowed to testify that he informed Thowsen the assault on Blaise was prior to Bailey's murder.

Stephen Pyszkowski

Blaise mentioned Stephen (Steve) Pyszkowski in her statement as someone she talked with after the attack on her. Thowsen interviewed him on July 23, 2001. He was called as a prosecution witness on the sixth day of Blaise's retrial.

Pyszkowski and his girlfriend, Kathy Renninger, let Blaise stay at their house during the month of June 2001. Instead of paying Pyszkowski, Blaise helped him for several weeks with his franchise business of servicing portable fire extinguishers. His service route included zip code 89103, and the Nevada State Bank where Bailey was murdered is in that zip code. Kephart tried to imply a connection between Pyszkowski's route and Blaise having knowledge of where the Nevada State Bank was. However, Pyszkowski did not testify that the bank was one of his customers, and in fact he didn't even testify that he had ever driven by the bank while Blaise was with him. [180] On cross-examination Pyszkowski testified that his service territory was about 10 miles square (100 square miles) and most of the time he drove because Blaise didn't know where to go. [181]

It also came out on cross-examination that Thowsen and LaRochelle questioned Pyszkowski for an hour or more before they turned the tape recorder on, so the recorded portion of his statement was only about 15-minutes. [182] So some things he told the detectives weren't in his statement, including that Blaise moved back to Panaca a few days before the Fourth of July.

After being told by the detectives that Blaise had been arrested for a murder committed on July 8, Pyszkowski told them that their "timeline" was off for Blaise to have committed the crime, because she had told him about being assaulted more than a month before then. That portion of Pyszkowski's statement was ignored by Kephart, but the following exchange took place on cross-examination:

Q. During the recorded portion of the statement when the police interviewed you, and your prior testimony, you told them their timeline was off, is that correct?
A. Yes, I mentioned that to them.
Q. What did you mean by that?
A. Well, they were asking me questions about – about Blaise staying over at the house, and they had mentioned something that had happened on a certain date, And I said well, you know, Blaise was living with me the month before that happened. And I had mentioned that those two dates didn't line up, that —
Q. The police came to talk to you about an incident that happened July 8, 2001, the murder of Duran Bailey, is that correct?

A. Yes.

Q. You told the police you had heard about an attack on Blaise the month before, correct?

Mr. Kephart: Your Honor, I'm gonna object on hearsay grounds.

...The Court: Counsel approach.

(Off-record bench conference from 11:13:00-11:15:06 a.m.)

The Court: The objection is sustained. [183]

By Ms. Greenberger:

Q. The information that you relayed to the police was derived, came from information you learned during the time period of June 2001, is that correct?

A. They were asking me about –

Mr. Kephart: Judge –

The Court: That calls for a yes or no.

The Witness: Okay. Please ask the question again. I'm sorry.

By Ms. Greenberger:

Q. Certainly. The information that you discussed with the police –

A. Mm-hmm.

Q – was information that came from June 2001, is that correct?

A. Yes.

Q. Were the police suggesting to you that you might be mistaken on your time period?

Mr. Kephart: Your Honor, I'm gonna object as to hearsay.

The Court: Sustained. [184]

Knowing that Vega wasn't going to allow Pyszkowski to explain anything about what Blaise told him about the May attack, the defense went on to question him about other matters.

The irony of Vega's rulings was that during Blaise's May 2002 trial, Pyszkowski was allowed to provide details about what Blaise told him that he was blocked from testifying about during her retrial. Among that testimony from 2002 is:

Q. Good afternoon, Mr. Pyszkowski. When you first spoke to the cops [Thowsen] and gave that taped statement that Mr. Kephart just showed you, you realized back then that the cops' time line was off, didn't you?

A. Yeah, I think I even mentioned it to them that they told me the approximate dates of when this incident happened and I said, well, I heard about it months before that.

Q. Okay.

A. At least a month before that.

...

(There are then a number of objections to Navarro's questions by Kephart on hearsay grounds that Judge Vega sustained.) The following exchange took place after a question by Navarro as to when he learned about an attack on Blaise:

A. In June.

Q. And how do you know that this was back in June?

A. I didn't see Blaise any time after the first of July until now. And she – when she left my house to stay with Doug she visited one time and I believe that was on the 2nd of July or around there. The weekend prior to the 4th of July. That was the last time I saw her. And I haven't seen her since then until today.

Q. And when you realized that you had already heard about this back in June, you told the police that?

A. Yes, I did. [185]

Thus the jury during Blaise's retrial didn't hear Pyszkowski testify that he knew in June that Blaise had been assaulted, and that is why three days after Blaise's arrest he told detective Thowsen his "timeline" was off for Blaise to have been involved in Bailey's murder.

Heather McBride

Heather McBride was an acquaintance of Blaise's who lived in Caliente. During Blaise's May 2002 trial McBride was called as a witness by the prosecution. She testified that on the evening of July 2 or 3, Blaise visited her. The following was her testimony on direct examination about that conversation:

Q. ... Do you recall anything specific about the conversation you had with her?
A. She told me that she'd stabbed somebody in the ab, abdomen.
Q. How did that come about?
A. We were – she was talking about when she was down here in Vegas, how she'd been staying here. [186]

...

Q. Okay. So, do you remember the exact word she used when she was describing what happened?
A. That someone had done her wrong and she had stabbed him in the abdomen, I have a problem saying that, and I'd asked if he had died? And she said she didn't know, she didn't stick around to find out. [187]

...

Q. Well, I mean did you believe her when she said that she had stabbed someone in the abdomen?
A. No, I didn't.
Q. Why didn't you?
A. Because she tends to exaggerate. [188]

The following exchange occurred during McBride's cross-examination by public defender Navarro:

Q. But she told you this before the 4th of July?
A. Yes.
Q. After the 1st of July?
A. Yes.
Q. And she told you that she cut him in the abdomen?
A. Yes
Q. Not in the penis?
A. Not in the penis, no. [189]

The jury during Blaise's retrial didn't hear that testimony from McBride that nearly a week before Bailey's murder, Blaise had told her that while in Las Vegas she fended off a man's attack by stabbing him in the abdomen (Which is a relatively common type of stabbing wound.), and that she had told that to Detectives Thowsen and LaRochelle on July 26, 2001. McBride testified as a defense witness and Judge Vega sustained the prosecutor's repeated objections during McBride's direct examination that her testimony about the assault was hearsay, and furthermore, the judge sustained as hearsay *anything* that she told the detectives during her interview. The following exchanges took place during McBride's direct examination by Greenberger:

By Ms. Greenberger:
Q. Without telling us what was said during your conversation, can you tell us what the subject of the conversation was?
Ms. DiGiacomo: Objection, hearsay.
The Court: Sustained. [190]

And,

By Ms. Greenberger:
Q. Did the police come talk to you in this case?
A. Yes.
Q. Was that on July 26, 2001?
A. Yeah.
Q. Did you come talk to you about a crime that had been committed?
A. Yes.
Q. When did you learn the crime had been committed?
Ms. DiGiacomo: Objection, leading.
The Court: Sustained.
By Ms. Greenberger:
Q. Do you know when the crime had been committed?
Ms. DiGiacomo: Objection, it's gonna call for a hearsay basis. And also vague as to what crime.
The Court: All right.
By Ms. Greenberger:
Q. What did the police come talk to you about?
Ms. DiGiacomo: Objection, hearsay.
The Court: Sustained.
By Ms. Greenberger:
Q. Did you make a statement to the police?
A. They recorded. There was a recorded statement made.
Q. Did you tell them everything you knew about this conversation you had with Blaise?
A. Yes, I did.
Q. Did you previously –
Ms. DiGiacomo: Objection, leading.
The Court: Sustained.
By Ms. Greenberger:
Q. Did you testify in a proceeding in this matter?
Ms. DiGiacomo: Objection, leading and relevance.
The Court: Sustained. [191]

Map of the Panaca neighborhood where Blaise and some of her alibi witnesses lived. See Table 3, p. 57.

Blaise's car parked on Callaway from July 2 to July 20, 2001

Michelle Austria's house

Open desert where Blaise and Michelle 4-wheeled on July 8

Gentry Rd

6th St

Lee Ct

Callaway Rd

McCrosky's house   Lobato's house   Jo Ann Dennert's house

After one more question Greenberger ended her direct examination. DiGiacomo's fourth cross-examination question was:

Q. All right. Do you recall testifying at a prior proceeding in May 2002?
A. Yes. [192]

DiGiacomo proceeded to elicit responses from McBride to a series of questions about Blaise's demeanor during her conversation with Blaise in early July 2001, and the statement she gave to Thowsen on July 26. On re-direct examination Vega then upheld DiGiacomo's objections that questions related to McBride's police statement and her conversation with Blaise were hearsay. Vega's sustaining of DiGiacomo's objections to questioning McBride about the very conversation and statement that she had allowed DiGiacomo to question her about created a bit of drama outside the jury's presence. Schieck argued on the record that the prosecution had brought McBride's statement into play, and under the "doctrine of completeness," [193] the defense had a right to question McBride about her statement in which days before Bailey's murder, she described Blaise telling her she had been attacked in Las Vegas. [194] Shari Greenberger said of the prosecution's fevered efforts to block the jury from hearing that prior to Bailey's murder Blaise had told McBride (and others) that she had been assaulted in Las Vegas, "I just want to memorialize the fact that the prosecution did illicit this very testimony on direct examination at the prior trial in this case." [195]

Greenberger also commented that justice wasn't being served by blocking the jury from hearing the truthful and relevant testimony of witnesses who could establish Blaise's absolute innocence. (The prosecution didn't even intimate that McBride and the other witnesses were not telling the truth about their conversations with Blaise prior to July 8 about the attack on her.) "And it is, you know, our contention we just want the truth to get out there. ... All we're seeking for is to get the truth out there through every and any witness that can provide any information." [196]

In a direct jab at Vega, that the judge was making prosecution favorable evidentiary rulings, Greenberger said, "Well, it's unfortunate that the rules of evidence in this case prevent the truth from coming out." [197]

After returning from lunch Vega reacted to Greenberger's comments about the injustice being inflicted on Blaise by the judge's evidentiary rulings barring the jury from hearing McBride's truthful testimony, by launching into a colloquiality about the virtues of the United States' legal system. [198]

Larry Lobato

Blaise's dad, Larry, went to Las Vegas in the last week of June 2001, and he had lunch with her before he returned to Panaca, Blaise told him that she had been assaulted around Memorial Day. During Blaise's May 2002 trial her lawyers didn't call Larry as a witness. He was called as a witness by the defense during Blaise's retrial. During Larry's direct examination Greenberger asked him if he spoke to Blaise when she was arrested at the family's home on July 20. He responded, "she told me she had done something that she had told me before in June." [199] After Kephart requested a bench conference, Vega upheld Kephart's objection to Larry answer as non-responsive to Greenberger's question.

Larry also testified that he talked with Thowsen after his wife Becky learned from the July 25 article in the Las Vegas *Review-Journal* that Blaise had been arrested for a murder committed on July 8. The following exchange occurred between Greenberger and Larry:

Q. As a result of information learned in the news article did you contact Detective Thowsen?
A. I did.
Q. What did you tell him?
A. I told him that he had the wrong person because the dates didn't match –
Q. What –
A. – cause Blaise was home on the 8th and that there was no way she could have been in Las Vegas at that time.
Q. What was his response?
Mr. Kephart: I'm going to object as to hearsay.
The Court: Sustained. [200]

Larry also testified that he talked with Thowsen at least one other time that he had arrested the wrong person because Blaise had been in Panaca on July 8:

Q. Did you ever talk to either of the homicide detectives again after that?
A. I believe I did in reference to her automobile.
Q. What did you talk to them about at that time?
A. Well, after we talked again about the dates being different I asked him if they had found any evidence in her car. He said no. I said, I guess than you can release it to me than.
Q. Was the car in fact released to you?
A. Yes, it was.
Q. And approximately what were the dates of these two conversations?
A. I would say the 28th and maybe the 30th. ...
Q. Of what month?
A. July.
Q. Of what year?
A. 2001. [201]

Since Thowsen had been directly informed that both Larry and Becky Lobato had information critical to the investigation of Bailey's murder, Larry was then asked by Greenberger:

Q. Did the police ever formally interview you on this case?
A. No.
Q. Not at any time?
A. No, they didn't interview me at all. [202]

That testimony was remarkable because Thowsen knew the day of Blaise's arrest that the butterfly knife she described as using to fend off her attacker, and which he believed was a weapon involved in stabbing Bailey, was given to her as a gift by her father, Larry. Blaise was charged, prosecuted and tried on the basis of that butterfly knife being one of the murder weapons. Yet neither Thowsen, LaRochelle, nor any other police investigator made any attempt to informally or formally question Larry about the knife (or any other information he might know). Thowsen made no attempt to acquire information from Larry (or Becky or Ashley Lobato) even when he returned to Panaca six days after Blaise's arrest to interview Dixie Tienken and several other people.

Larry made two critical points when he testified about his methamphetamine use from 1998 to 2002: [203]

Q. (by Greenberger) When you were using methamphetamine, did you get it in Lincoln County?
A. Yes. [204]

Larry also testified:

Q. (cross-examination by Kephart) Okay. Methamphetamine is something that you crave all the time, you want it all the time?
A. Not necessarily. [205]

Both of those answers undermined two critical components of the prosecution's theory of the crime: That Blaise drove to Las Vegas because she couldn't get methamphetamines locally, and that as a methamphetamine user she was so insane with craving that she drove to Las Vegas in the middle of the night on July 6 to get the drug, and than returned to Panaca in the early morning of July 8. (The prosecution never attempted to explain why Blaise did not exhibit any signs of recent drug use in Panaca that morning.) Although Larry Lobato's responses were the only information provided during the trial related to and undermining those two critical aspects of the prosecution's case, as will be seen, defense attorney Schieck made no mention of either in his closing argument. (Neither did Schieck, during his cross-examination of Laura Johnson, question her about the availability of methamphetamines (and other drugs) in Lincoln County, even though Johnson told Thowsen in her statement of July 20, 2001 that drugs were available locally.)

Additionally, Larry testified that he talked with Blaise on the morning of July 8 after he got home from work between midnight and 1 a.m., [206] and that after watching television for a while he went to bed about 2 am, and passed Blaise while she was sleeping on the futon in the living room. [207]

Michelle Austria

Michelle Austria lived in Panaca near the Lobato's house. Austria and Blaise were friends who talked and went four-wheeling together. During Blaise's retrial (and also during her May 2002 trial) Austria was called as a witness by the prosecution. Austria testified that on a day around the Fourth of July 2001 Blaise told her about fending off an assault in Las Vegas. Austria also testified that she was alone with Blaise when this conversation took place. [208] However, the prosecution elicited Austria testimony with the intention it would benefit their case, because the next prosecution witness was her boyfriend Paul "Rusty" Brown. He testified that he was present for part of the conversation between Blaise and Austria, and he thought it occurred about a week before Blaise's arrest, which would have been after Bailey's murder. [209] Thus the only testimony allowed by Vega related to Blaise telling people about the assault was from Austria, and the prosecution wanted Brown's testimony to suggest to the jury that Austria could have been told about it after Bailey was murdered. However, Austria's testimony about when the conversation occurred was consistent with what she told Thowsen in a taped statement on July 26, 2001, six days after Blaise's arrest. The following is an excerpt from Austria's testimony on direct examination about the conversation she had with Blaise:

Q. You're not positive of the date that this occurred?
A. I do – no,
Q. But you believe it was sometime around the 4th of July, that's your –
A. Yes.
Q. And what was the conversation that you had with Blaise?
A. Well, she talked to me about going down to Vegas. She was in Vegas and she had been attacked by somebody, and she proceeded to grab onto him and slash at his penis.
Q. Did she say how she got a knife?
A. She had it on her.
Q. And she said this happened in Las Vegas?
A. Yes.
Q. Do you get more specific about where it happened?
A. No.
Q. Did she give more specifics about what happened, how she was attacked?
A. Just that this guy came onto her and attacked her. It's – I believe in a parking lot. That's all the information I have. We didn't go into detail about this.
Q. Did she tell you when it happened?
A. No.
...
Q. ... After reviewing your statement on page 9, does that refresh your recollection whether or not she did give you an indication of when it happened?

A. I was pretty much guessing on a time because that's when – in there it says I specify nighttime, that's because she was out and about, so that's –

Q. Well –

A. – why I specified night. [210]

Austria's direct testimony about her conversation with Blaise prior to Bailey's murder was consistent with Blaise's statement on four significant details: Blaise was assaulted sometime prior to July 2001, she slashed at her attacker's penis, the assault occurred in a parking lot, and it happened at night. On cross-examination by defense lawyer Greenberger it was further clarified that the assault Blaise told her about didn't resemble the details of Bailey's murder, and that it was common for women (and men) from Panaca to carry a knife:

Q. So if we look at Defendant's JJ (Poster sized calendar), you took that to mean sometime in June 2001 she was the victim of a prior attack?

A. Yes.

Q. That's accurate?

A. Yes.

Q. Did she also tell you that she defended herself?

A. Yes.

Q. And she got away?

A. Yes.

A. It is true.

Q. It is true that she never told you —

A. She never specified –

Q. – that she actually stabbed him?

A. – that she actually stabbed him.

Q. She never told you that she punched someone, did she?

A. No.

Q. She never told you that she stabbed someone in the carotid artery, did she?

A. No,

Q. She never told you that she brutally beat a man and gave him two black eyes, did she?

A. No.

Q. She never told you that she cut someone's penis off after the man was dead, did she?

A. No.

Q. She never told you that she slashed the man's rear that attacked her?

A. No.

Q. She never told you that she hit the man that attacked her with a baseball bat, did she?

A. No,

Q. You would remember these things, would you?

A. Yeah, I would remember all of those things

Q. And as you sit here today, you can tell the ladies and gentlemen of the jury with certainty that she never told you any of those things, isn't that true?

A. Yes, it is.

Q. With regard to a butterfly knife in Panaca, pretty common?

A. Yes.

Q. In fact, you yourself carry a knife, true, or at the time?

A. At the time. I mean pocketknife.

Q. For what reason?

A. Just to have on you in case you need it, you know. When you're out four-wheeling, you know, you never know if you're gonna need it for something or – it's just not a – it's a common thing to have a knife on you.

Q. Is it equally common for men and women, as far as you know?

A. Yes,

Q. Do many girlfriends of yours, or at the time, carried knives?

A. As far as I know, yeah.

Q. So it's not unusual to you —

A. No, it's not unusual.

Q. – that someone would be walking around with a knife?

A. No. [211]

Alibi witnesses

Fourteen people testified that they saw Blaise in Panaca between July 2 and July 9. [212] Eleven of those people testified they saw her on the weekend of July 7 and 8. All of the relatives, acquaintances, and neighbors who also testified about seeing Blaise's car parked in front of her parents house said they never saw it moved or parked in a different position on the city street behind a utility trailer, after she arrived from Las Vegas on July 2, until the police took it away on July 20. Two of the people testifying about Blaise's parked car were the Lobato's next door neighbors, Robert and Wanda McCrosky, a married couple that had lived in Panaca for 40 years and 75 years respectively. [213]

Using a poster sized calendar, Blaise's lawyers asked each witness to sign their initials on the days they saw Blaise in Panaca. At the end of this chapter is a table of Blaise's alibi witnesses from July 2 to July 9. (Table 3)

Kristina Paulette

During LVMPD Crime Lab technician Kristina Paulette's testimony on September 25, 2006 as a prosecution witness, she described the DNA test results of a pubic hair combed from Bailey's public hair that remained untested in Bailey's rape kit for more than five years. The test not only excluded Blaise, but it was identified as originating from an unknown male.

After the retrial began DiGiacomo secretly instructed the crime lab to perform DNA testing of three cigarette butts found on Bailey's body. The test report was issued two days after Paulette testified for the prosecution, so she was called as a defense witness on October 2. She testified that one butt did not have isolatable DNA, another had Bailey's DNA (from his blood) and the DNA of an unidentifiable person, and the third only had the DNA of an unidentified male. She also testified the DNA on the second and third butts originated from different persons. Paulette testified that Blaise was conclusively excluded as a source of the DNA on the second and third cigarette butts. Those exclusionary results were particularly important because Blaise smoked cigarettes in July 2001 when Bailey was murdered.

Although Paulette may have a level of expertise in testing for the presence of DNA, her lack of awareness about the value of DNA for identification purposes was revealed by her response to a question by DiGiacomo that went unchallenged by Blaise's lawyers. Paulette responded "Absolutely not.", in response to DiGiacomo's question, "Now the fact that you find a person's DNA on an item you tested, that doesn't tell you whether or not they did the crime, correct?" [214] Paulette's answer was intellectually indefensible. Consider the following scenario: A woman reports that a lone man who didn't use a condom raped her, and all the proper protocols are followed in immediately collecting the rapist's sperm for her rape kit. A suspect is arrested and his DNA profile is established to have an extraordinarily high probability of matching the lone DNA profile detected from the rape kit's sperm sample. Even though to a near scientific certainty that suspect is identified as the woman's lone assailant, based on Paulette's testimony in Blaise's trial, her opinion is the scientific evidence is relatively unimportant in establishing his guilt. In actual practice the DNA linking the man to the rape would, along with the woman's testimony, be the centerpiece of the prosecution's case against him. Yet Blaise's attorneys didn't cross-examine Paulette about her inaccurate testimony about the unimportance of DNA evidence to establish culpability, and conversely, to absolve a person of being a crime's perpetrator. So the jury was left with the impression that the cigarette butts found directly on Bailey's body underneath the plastic sheeting wrapped around his body had little or no value in identifying his killer(s) – who were presumably the male and other person who smoked those cigarettes. Paulette's testimony also led the jury to believe that the cigarette butts had little or no value in excluding Blaise of murdering Bailey – even though she was a smoker.

That Paulette will testify falsely for the benefit of her "home" team and employer – the LVMPD – was amply illustrated when she falsely testified on September 25 that she wasn't conducting any tests on evidence in Blaise's case, even though she was secretly testing the cigarette butts at DiGiacomo's direction. DiGiacomo remained silent during Paulette's false testimony and didn't bring her possible perjury to Judge Vega's attention. When Paulette testified on October 2 about the cigarette butt DNA test results, she admitted testifying on September 25 that no further tests were being conducted.

Inconsistencies in the prosecution's case

When the presentation of evidence was completed on October 5, 2006 there were a number of glaring inconsistencies in the prosecution's case against Blaise and what was known about Bailey's life and the circumstances of his death. Fourteen of those are explained in Table 4 (p. 60).

These were not trivial problems with the prosecution's case, but they were central to their allegation that Blaise murdered and then sexually assaulted Bailey after he died.

Among the inconsistencies was the absence of any evidence establishing a motive for Blaise to have been at Bailey's "home" in the Nevada State Bank's trash enclosure, and even further, there was no evidence that Blaise had ever been to that bank, that she had ever met Bailey or knew who he was, or that she even knew anyone who knew him. In addition there was no evidence establishing that Blaise had been anywhere in Las Vegas on July 8, or that refuted the defense's alibi evidence that Blaise and her car had been in Panaca the entire day of Bailey's death. Furthermore, Blaise was excluded as a suspect by all the conclusively tested crime scene evidence that included fingerprints, bloody shoeprints, DNA testing of chewing gum, a pubic hair, and cigarette butts, and her cars tire treads didn't match those found next to the trash enclosure. Additionally, Blaise had no injuries, particularly to her hands, that Bailey's assailant(s) would be expected to have suffered, and both the prosecution expert Simms, and the defense expert Turvey agreed that Bailey's distinctive injuries suggested his death had homosexual overtones. On top of those inconsistencies, Bailey lost about two quarts of blood, but none of his blood was found in Blaise's car, on the baseball bat she kept in her car for self-protection, or on any other item of hers.

Consequently, at the point closing arguments began, the inconsistencies in the prosecution's case made it plain that they had presented no evidence establishing that Blaise had the motive, means, opportunity, or even any possibility of intent to have murdered Bailey – a man who based on the evidence she had never met.

Table 3
Alibi Timeline Of Blaise's Continuous Presence In Panaca From July 2 to July 9

Person	Event	Time
July 2 – Monday	Doug Twining (boyfriend) sees Blaise off as she leaves Las Vegas for her parent's house in Panaca.	Noon
	Drives from Las Vegas to her parent's home in Panaca in her 1984 Fiero. Her dad Larry Lobato, mom Becky Lobato and sister Ashley were home when she arrived.	Afternoon/ Evening
	Clint Holman (friend) sees Blaise at the Panaca Mini-Mart, where he worked.	4 p.m.
	Chris Carrington sees and briefly talks with Blaise at gas station in Caliente.	Evening
	Blaise visits Heather McBride's (friend) house in Caliente and they talk for 1 to 2 hours. (On either July 2 or 3). Chris Collier, McBride's boyfriend, was home and talked with Blaise.	Evening
	Doug Twining called Blaise twice from Las Vegas (per phone records).	Evening
July 3 – Tuesday	Blaise sleeps much of the day and is lethargic. Her mom, dad and sister see her at home.	Various
	Blaise visits Heather McBride's house in Caliente and they talk for 1 to 2 hours. (On either July 2 or 3). Chris Collier, McBride's boyfriend, was home and talked with Blaise.	Evening
	Doug Twining called Blaise twice from Las Vegas (per phone records).	Late afternoon
July 4 – Wednesday	4th of July barbecue in backyard of Blaise's parents house. Numerous relatives, friends and neighbors see Blaise. She is lethargic and sleeps much of the day.	Various
	Doug Twining called Blaise twice from Las Vegas (per phone records).	Morning and afternoon
July 5 – Thursday	Blaise's mom, dad and sister Ashley see her at various times during the day and evening.	Early morning to evening
	Chris Carrington (friend) visited the Lobato house and talked with Blaise while he used exercise equipment in the garage.	Afternoon
	Blaise is still lethargic so late in the afternoon her mom takes her to the Caliente Clinic to see a doctor late in the afternoon. Records show a blood sample was drawn from Blaise at 5:15 p.m. that tested negative for methamphetamines, when tested by a Las Vegas lab on July 7, 2001.[215]	Late afternoon
	Doug Twining called Blaise once from Las Vegas (per phone records).	Evening
July 6 – Friday	Mom calls in to take the day off from work to stay with Blaise and begins to collect her urine in container per doctor's instructions.	6 a.m.
	Robert McCrosky (next door neighbor to the right of the Lobato's) sees Blaise's car parked on the street in front of the Lobato house as he takes his early morning walk.	Early morning
	Wanda McCrosky (neighbor and wife of Robert) saw Blaise's car when she went outside or looked outside.	Early morning to evening
	Blaise's dad and sister Ashley see her at various times during the day and evening.	Various
	Chris Carrington visited the Lobato house and talked with Blaise while he used exercise equipment in the garage.	Afternoon
	Doug Twining called Blaise twice from Las Vegas (per phone records).	Evening
July 7 – Saturday	Mom leaves for work in Caliente while Blaise is sleeping on the futon in the living room, and drops off Blaise's 24-hour urine sample at the Caliente Clinic.	6:50 a.m.
	Robert McCrosky sees Blaise's car parked on the street in front of the Lobato house as he takes his early morning walk.	Early morning

Table 3 (Continued)

Person	Event	Time
	Wanda McCrosky sees Blaise's car when she went outside or looked outside.	Early morning to evening
	Ashley sees Blaise at various times during the day and evening.	Various
	Dad leaves for work and Blaise is home.	3 p.m.
	Chris Carrington visited the Lobato house and talked with Blaise while he used exercise equipment in the garage.	Afternoon
	Blaise's grandfather talked with her when he returned a call by her dad earlier in the day. (It was her grandfather's birthday.)	3 to 4 p.m.
	Becky calls home and tells Blaise she is stopping by Larry's work in Caliente on her way home from work.	4 to 4:15 p.m.
	Michelle Austria (friend and the Lobato's neighbor across the street) and her boyfriend Paul "Rusty" Brown pick-up Blaise and they all drive to Caliente. [216]	4:30 p.m.
	Michelle, Rusty and Blaise pick-up Mike (friend) at his work in Caliente, and they all go to the restaurant/bar where Blaise's dad worked in Caliente.	5 p.m.
	Blaise calls her mom and asks her to pick her up in Caliente at the restaurant/bar.	9:35 p.m.
	Becky picks up Blaise in Caliente.	10 p.m.
	Doug Twining called Blaise four times from Las Vegas. (per phone records).	Evening
July 8 – Sunday	Larry Lobato arrives home from work between Midnight and 1 a.m. – Blaise is lying on the living room futon and they talk for a bit. Larry watches television and when he goes to bed at 2 a.m. Blaise is asleep on the futon.	Midnight to 2 a.m.
	Becky Lobato gets up for work (5:45 a.m.) and Blaise is asleep on the living room futon, where she still is when she leaves for work (6:50 a.m.).	5:45 to 6:50 a.m.
	John Kraft (cousin) is scheduled to leave for a job in Minnesota in a couple of days, and he comes over to the Lobato home to talk to Larry about watching his family while he is away. Blaise answers the door in her pajamas – John later said she was sleepy like he had woken her up.	7 a.m.
	Larry Lobato sees Blaise when she wakes him up to let him know that John Kraft wants to see him. Larry sees Blaise on the futon after talking with Kraft for 10 to 15 minutes.	7 to 7:15 a.m.
	Robert McCrosky sees Blaise's car parked on the street in front of the Lobato house as he takes his early morning walk.	Early morning
	Wanda McCrosky sees Blaise's car when she went outside or looked outside.	Early morning to evening
	Michelle Austria is 4-wheeling with Blaise and talked with her.	11:30 a.m.
	Clint Holman sees Blaise and Michelle Austria 4-wheeling in the desert area surrounding the Lobato house, while he was riding his horse after church.	11:30 a.m.
	Jo Ann Dennert (next door neighbor to the left of the Lobato's) watches Blaise 4-wheeling, while she is washing dishes.	11:00 a.m. to 1 p.m.
	Paul "Rusty" Brown sees Blaise. [217]	Late morning to early afternoon
	Larry Lobato sees Blaise before he leaves for work at the Hideway in Caliente.	3 to 3:30 p.m.
	Ashley Lobato saw Blaise during the day and evening, and she remembers seeing Blaise in the garage with Chris Carrington.	3 to 4 p.m.
	Chris Carrington visits the Lobato house and talked with Blaise while he uses exercise equipment in the garage.	4-6:45 p.m.[218]
	Becky Lobato (She got off work at 4 p.m. and when she got home she saw and talked with Blaise and Chris Carrington.)	4:20 p.m. to 1 a.m. (July 9)

Table 3 (Continued)

Person	Event	Time
	Kendre Thunstrom (neighbor on adjoining street) is riding with her boyfriend in his truck when it breaks down in front of the Lobato's house. Blaise is standing in the driveway, and the two of talk them for 30-45 minutes while Thunstrom's boyfriend fixes the truck.	5 to 6 p.m.
	Shane Kraft (cousin) visits Lobato house and talks with Blaise, Becky and Ashley.	6 to 8 p.m.
	John Kraft (Shane's husband) visits Lobato house and talks with Blaise, Becky and Ashley.	8 p.m.
	Chris Carrington visits and sees Blaise packing to return to Las Vegas	10 p.m.
	Doug Twining calls Blaise five times from Las Vegas or on the way to Panaca from Las Vegas (per phone records). The first call was at 9:09 a.m.	Morning and Evening
July 9 – Monday	Ashley says good-bye to Blaise as she is packing to go to Las Vegas with her friend Doug Twining, who was driving to Panaca to pick her up.	12:20 a.m.
	Becky Lobato sees Blaise leave for Las Vegas with Twining.	12:30 – 1 a.m.
	Larry Lobato, after arriving home from work, sees Blaise leave for Las Vegas with Twining.	12:30 – 1 a.m.
	Twining arrives in Panaca from Las Vegas to take Blaise back to Las Vegas with him. Telephone records confirm that Twining made three phone calls on the evening of July 8 and one during the early morning of July 9 while driving to Panaca and to get directions to the Lobato house, where he had never been before. Blaise's mom and dad are up when she leaves with Doug.	12:30 – 1 a.m.
July 9 to July 13 - Monday to Friday	Blaise stays with Twining at his parent's house in Las Vegas. Doug later testifies that they smoked marijuana, but didn't take any methamphetamines during the week.	
July 13 – Friday	Blaise's dad drives to Las Vegas to pick-up Blaise and bring her back to Panaca	

Table 4
14 Inconsistencies Between Facts of Bailey's Murder and his Behavior and Blaise
(Not considering the differences between Blaise's statement and the facts of Bailey's murder.
See Tables 1 and 2 for those differences.)

Inconsistency	Bailey	Blaise
Drug motive	Regular crack cocaine user, and cocaine was in his system at his time of death. He didn't use methamphetamines.	Used methamphetamines in Las Vegas. There was no evidence she had ever used crack cocaine, and no traces were found in her car.
Geographical	Murdered in a Nevada State Bank's trash enclosure on Las Vegas' west side.	No witness, surveillance video, bank receipt, or other evidence that Blaise had ever at any time been to the Nevada State Bank.
Bloody shoeprints	Bloody shoeprints leading away from Bailey's body were made by a man's size 9 athletic shoe.	Wears size 7-1/2 woman's shoe, equal to man's size 6 to 6-1/2.
DNA evidence	Bailey's DNA is on crime scene evidence.	No crime scene evidence has Blaise's DNA, and none of Blaise's personal items or her car has any of Bailey's DNA.
Blood evidence	Bailey lost two quarts of blood at the crime scene. Bloody shoeprints were both leading away from his body, and on the cardboard on top of his body.	None of Bailey's blood was found on any personal item of Blaise or in her car.
Baseball Bat	Simms testified that Bailey's injuries were inconsistent with being caused by a baseball bat.	Blaise kept a baseball bat in her car for self-defense that tested negative for the presence of any blood.
Tire treads	A set of undisturbed tire tracks was found next to the trash enclosure where Bailey's body was found.	The tires on Blaise's car don't match the crime scene tire tracks.
Injuries	Beaten severely. Stabbed multiple times prior to and after death. Penis severed and anus cut after death.	Blaise had no injuries to her hands, or elsewhere on her body attributable to violently assaulting a person – such as Bailey was assaulted.
Eyewitnesses	No witness to Bailey's murder has come forward.	Eleven alibi witnesses saw or talked with Blaise in Panaca on July 8 from about 12:30 a.m. until after Bailey's body was first seen by the police at 10:50 p.m.
Homosexual overtones	Sexual mutilation of Bailey after his death was described by M. E. Simms and defense expert Turvey as associated with male homosexuality. Simms testified that none of the dozen or cases of male mutilation after death that he had personal experience with involved a woman, and he had never heard or read of any such case in the professional literature. Turvey wrote in his pre-trial report that researching male mutilation after death resulted in him finding only one that allegedly involved a woman – Blaise's case.	Blaise is a woman.
Time of death	Although Simms has given four different times of death for Bailey that range from about 10:30 p.m. to 3:50 a.m. – the common denominator of all of them is that Bailey died on July 8.	Eleven alibi witnesses saw or talked with Blaise in Panaca on July 8 from about 12:30 a.m. until after Bailey's body was first seen by the police at 10:50 p.m. Two other alibi witnesses said that they didn't see Blaise's car moved on July 8.

Table 4 (Continued)

Inconsistency	Bailey	Blaise
Location	Murdered in Las Vegas on July 8.	No evidence of any kind – no eyewitness, surveillance video, gas receipt, etc. – that Blaise was in Las Vegas on July 8 (or on July 6 or 7).
Personally acquainted	A person or persons acquainted with Bailey murdered him based on the expert opinion of Simms and Turvey that the crime scene and Bailey's injuries strongly suggest homosexual overtones.	No evidence that Blaise knew Bailey – or had ever had any contact of any kind with him.
Circle of acquaintances	People in the area of the Nevada State Bank were acquainted with Bailey, and these people included Richard Shott (who discovered Bailey's body), Diann Parker (who was raped and beaten by Bailey), and the Mexicans (who warned Bailey to stay away from Parker).	No evidence that Blaise knew any of Bailey's circle of acquaintances, or even that any of Blaise's Las Vegas acquaintances knew Bailey or any of his circle of acquaintances.

VI
Closing Arguments and Verdict

The personality differences between the two prosecutors and Blaise's lawyer conducting the closing, David Schieck, were stark. Prosecutor DiGiacomo has the bearing and mannerisms of a spoiled, petulant child. Prosecutor Kephart has a forceful personality and the mannerisms of a snake-oil salesman. While Schieck has the earnest, low key manner of a college professor.

DiGiacomo's closing argument

DiGiacomo's closing revolved around the theme: It is possible Blaise killed Bailey. Among DiGiacomo's speculations were:

• It is possible there was someone's blood in Blaise's car – even though the confirmatory forensic tests were negative for the presence of any blood.

• It is possible there was someone's blood on her bat – even though forensic tests were negative for blood.

• It is possible her car was at the scene of Bailey's murder – even though the tire tracks next to the crime scene didn't match her car, numerous eyewitnesses said her car was not moved in Panaca from July 2 to July 20, no witness saw her car in Las Vegas on July 8, and no witness saw her car being driven in either direction between Panaca and Las Vegas at any time after July 2.

• It is possible she left Panaca on Friday, July 6 for Las Vegas to obtain methamphetamines, and it is possible she was in Las Vegas on the very early morning of July 8 – even though during the four week-long trial, the prosecution presented no evidence refuting the testimony of Blaise's alibi witnesses that she and her car were in Panaca on July 6, 7 and 8. [219] (See Table 3, p. 57.) Furthermore, no one testified to seeing Blaise or her car in Las Vegas on July 6, 7 or 8, and there is no eyewitness or surveillance video from any gas station or convenience store placing Blaise or her car anywhere in the 170 miles between Panaca/Caliente and Las Vegas on July 6, 7 or 8.

DiGiacomo's speculation that its "possible" Blaise made the 340 mile round-trip to Las Vegas to obtain methamphetamine from Bailey also disregarded that prior to Blaise's arrest Laura Johnson told Thowsen in her statement on July 20, 2001, that methamphetamine was available in Lincoln County, and Larry Lobato testified that during the five years (1998-2002) he used methamphetamines he obtained the drug locally in Lincoln County. [220]

DiGiacomo did not even attempt to reconcile her it is "possible" argument with the fact that the prosecution presented no evidence to rebut Blaise's statement that "from about a week before then [the attack on her] till about a week, a week afterwards, I was out of my mind on drugs. ... Methamphetamines, staying up for days and days at a time." [221] Her description fits her lifestyle at the end of May in 2001, but not in July. A lab's analysis of Blaise's blood sample taken at the Caliente Clinic at 5:15 p.m. on July 5 tested negative for methamphetamines, the unrebutted testimony by numerous witnesses is Blaise was lethargic and tired for days after arriving in Panaca on July 2, and her mom took July 6 off from work to stay home and care for Blaise. In addition the unrebutted testimony of Doug Twining was that after returning to Las Vegas on July 9, all he and Blaise did was smoke some marijuana until her dad picked her up and took her back to Panaca on July 13. The prosecution did not present *any* evidence that Blaise took *any* methamphetamines for a week prior to and a week after July 8 – which supports that the assault she described in her statement was a different event than Bailey's murder.

• It is possible Blaise went to the trash enclosure to get methamphetamines from Bailey – even though witnesses testified he used crack cocaine and he didn't use methamphetamines (cocaine and alcohol was in his system at the time of his death), no one testified he had ever sold any drugs, and no witness testified Blaise had ever met or knew of the homeless Bailey, or that she had ever been to the Nevada State Bank where he lived in the trash enclosure.

• It is possible that the crime scene evidence that wasn't collected, preserved and/or tested by the Metro PD did not support that Blaise wasn't Bailey's murderer, because if it had been collected, preserved and tested it might have identified that she was in fact present — which suggested to the jury that the prosecution did not have the burden to present evidence proving Blaise's guilt beyond a reasonable doubt. [222]

To support her it is "possible" she did it claim, DiGiacomo speculated about numerous allegations that were either unsupported by any trial evidence or directly contradictory to the trial evidence. While normally called "facts" not in evidence, DiGiacomo's arguments were based on pure speculation that had no relationship to "facts." Consequently, DiGiacomo's closing was not based on the reality of the evidence presented during Blaise's trial – but was constructed from the whole cloth of speculation about unproven and illogical, if not downright impossible "possibilities." She even had a PowerPoint presentation laying out her speculation that Blaise was Bailey's killer. [223] DiGiacomo made her factually deficient arguments without caution or restraint, and with few objections by Blaise's lawyers.

Schieck's closing argument

Schieck's closing was built on several interrelated themes: Much crime scene evidence that Bailey's killer(s) likely handled either wasn't collected or tested; crime scene evidence that was collected and tested excludes Blaise; there is nothing in her statement that incriminates her in Bailey's murder; nothing in her possession or her car links her to Bailey's murder; the unrebutted alibi testimony of nearly a dozen people establishes she was in Panaca the entire day of July 8; and because of the complete absence of inculpatory evidence, the prosecution was seeking to have Blaise convicted on their speculation it was possible she killed Bailey – and not proof beyond a reasonable doubt.

Schieck argued that the prosecution's case was built on a whole series of "possibilities" and maybes and supposes, precisely because there is no evidence whatsoever that Blaise was involved in any way with Bailey's murder, or even that she was within 170 miles of the crime scene. He variously described the prosecution's case as, "It's possible it happened this way," "somehow this came to pass," "somehow Blaise came into contact with Mr. Bailey," "somehow Mr. Bailey had Drugs," "somehow there was a sex for drugs thing going on," "Somehow, somehow, somehow, it goes on and on."

Schieck reminded the jury that over and over the prosecution asked witnesses "Isn't it possible?", after their testimony didn't fit the prosecution's scenario. He told the jury, "That is their case against Blaise Lobato, isn't it possible and somehow this happened."

Schieck explained that the prosecution was supporting their scenario of the crime with the argument, "There is nothing to disprove this so it must be true." He told the jurors, "The prosecution is actually defending themselves from the lack of evidence and trying to convince you that somehow they have proved anything in this case." Kephart objected to that statement, complaining to Vega, "He's disparaging the State."

Schieck continued, "Isn't it possible that she wasn't there and that's why they have no evidence? Isn't that more likely from a scientific standpoint to say that a lack of evidence speaks volumes in this case?"

He plainly asked the jury, "Isn't it possible they are prosecuting an innocent person? Isn't that a possibility if they want to talk about possibilities?"

Schieck emphasized, "What happened in this case is a snap judgment was made to arrest Blaise Lobato in Panaca, Nevada, and for the next five years the State and the detectives have attempted to prove their case after they made their arrest instead of doing it the right way of getting your facts straight before you arrest someone and charge them with murder."

He said of Thowsen after Blaise's arrest, "We've solved our case, we have someone in custody, we submit it to the DA to prosecute. Well maybe we should do some investigating. Now that we've made up our minds, maybe we should do some investigating. Maybe we should do some investigating to justify the arrest we've made."

Schieck lamented the failure of the police to collect, preserve or test the overwhelming amount of crime scene evidence likely handled by Bailey's killer(s), including the plastic sheeting wrapped around his body. He told the jury, "That plastic is in evidence. The plastic that you'll see was molded as if with hands around the body of the deceased person. To this day it has never been tested by anyone. It is in evidence. ... In all likelihood touched by the perpetrator. Never tested."

He encouraged the jurors to listen to Blaise's taped statement, telling them, "There is no evidence in that statement that is going to convict her in this case."

He also told the jury that when the defense presents an alibi defense, "the State has the burden of disproving the alibi." He then asked the jurors: "Have they presented any evidence, other than speculation, conjecture, and is it possible to disprove that Blaise was in Panaca at the time Duran Bailey was killed?"

Schieck also gave the jury a bit of a history lesson by telling them that the prosecutions burden of proving a defendant guilty beyond a reasonable doubt was embedded in the Bill of Rights to prevent a person such as Blaise from being convicted without evidence of her guilt. He explained, "The burden of proof is beyond a reasonable doubt, not, it's possible." [224]

Although any argument can be critiqued for what it didn't include, there was one very glaring omission from Schieck's argument: the importance of the semen recovered from Bailey's rectum. Even without being DNA tested, the detection of the semen offers powerful support for the expert testimony of Simms and Turvey that Bailey's murder was of the sort typically associated with homosexual activity – which explains the absence of evidence tying Blaise to the crime, and that her many unrebutted alibi witnesses place her in Panaca on July 8.

Kephart's rebuttal closing argument

Kephart is an experienced prosecutor who knows from more than 100 jury trials that evidence of a defendant's guilt isn't necessary to win a conviction, as long as he is able to push the jurors emotional buttons that make them bypass the thought process and feel a defendant is guilty without being able to coherently articulate why.

Since the prosecution had no substantive evidence upon which to base an argument for the jury to find Blaise guilty, Kephart resorted during his rebuttal to using his forceful personality to command the jury's attention while he made an emotion laden zealous argument for a guilty verdict based on the theme that it was too coincidental for a man to be non-fatally wounded by having his groin area stabbed or cut as Blaise described in her statement, and six weeks later for another man across town to have his penis severed after he was dead. Thus Kephart's argument was based on the assumption that the attack described by Blaise and Bailey's murder were the same event.

Using violent motions through the air with his arms and savage thrusts of his hands, Kephart evangelized that Blaise stabbed and beat Bailey while in a drug fueled rage at men for being raped when she was a little girl and twice as a teenager. The defense didn't object to Kephart's tirade, even though no evidence was presented that in July 2001 Blaise was suffering from incipient murderous rage towards men because of past events.

Kephart's argument bet that the middle-class jury could be induced to disregard that no evidence tied Blaise to Bailey's murder or even put her within 170 miles of the crime scene, if they could be convinced that in July 2001 she was a thoroughly bad and depraved young women who would do anything to satisfy what he alleged was her uncontrollable methamphetamine craving. Kephart's clear but unstated message to the straight-laced jurors was that Blaise should be convicted because she was a bad person who in the months prior to Bailey's murder had used methamphetamines and associated with people who also did so.

To deflect the juror's attention away from the prosecution's burden of proof, he emphasized as had DiGiacomo, that the absence of any crime scene evidence tying Blaise to Bailey's murder didn't mean that she wouldn't have been incriminated if all the evidence had been collected, preserved and tested by the Metro PD. [225]

Kephart's closing emotional appeal to the jury was showing them a large blow-up of Blaise's picture taken when she was arrested in Panaca on July 20. He thundered that the short-haired bleach blond 18-year-old with no make-up shown in the picture is who the jury was judging and should convict – not the attractive 23-year-old brunette with long "swept-back" hair sitting at the defense table. As with DiGiacomo's closing, the defense didn't object to many of Kephart's arguments that were not based on the trial evidence.

Kephart keyed on the juror's emotions

The degree to which Kephart pandered to the jurors emotions and sought for them to suspend rational thought, is illustrated by the way his arguments disregarded clearly exculpatory evidence, such as the tests that excluded Blaise as the source of DNA on two cigarette butts found on Bailey's body. (Blaise smoked in July 2001 but none of her cigarette butts were found at the crime scene.) One butt had the DNA of an unidentified male, and the other had Bailey's blood and the DNA profile of an unidentified person. So the success of Kephart's (and DiGiacomo's) argument depended on the jurors acceptance of the hypothetical scenario that after Blaise savagely murdered Bailey in a methamphetamine induced rage and cut off his penis, she hurriedly left the scene. Then, sometime afterward at least two people who had nothing to do with Bailey's murder, one of whom is known to be a male, somehow came upon Bailey's body that was concealed behind the dumpster in the trash enclosure. Those people then nonchalantly smoked cigarettes, then carefully placed the butts on Bailey's body, then carefully wrapped plastic sheeting around his body, being conscientious enough to neatly tuck the plastic underneath his body, and then they took the time to place a considerable pile of trash (presumably taken from the dumpster) on top of his body to conceal it from easy discovery. That scenario that unknown smokers who had nothing to do with Bailey's murder placed their cigarette butts on his body that they then wrapped in plastic and concealed under trash, at a minimum stretches credulity, and at a maximum is fantastic beyond belief, but in either case it is not supported by evidence presented by the prosecution during Blaise's trial. The logical conclusion is the smokers murdered Bailey. Yet Kephart (and DiGiacomo) had confidence from their experience that the jury would not summarily reject their scenario that diverted attention from the forensic, physical, documentary, medical, alibi and circumstantial evidence that excludes Blaise from involvement in the crime.

The jury was unaware that coincidences are the norm in life

Kephart argued to the jury that some details of Bailey's murder and the assault described by Blaise in her statement are too coincidental for them to be different events. The primary "detail" he considered as too much of a match to be coincidental was the careful amputation of Bailey's exposed penis by an unidentified sharp object after his death, and Blaise's description that in a frantic effort to get away from her black assailant she slashed with her knife at his exposed penis as he hovered above her. (Kephart, however, disregarded that Blaise described her attacker as very much alive when she got away from him and left in her car).

So the three undisputed similarities forming the core of Kephart's argument are the incidents involved a black male, an exposed penis, and a sharp object. It is not unusual for a rape or attempted rape in Las Vegas to involve those three things. In fact, all three were involved in Bailey's alleged rape of Diann Parker seven days before his murder.

Kephart disregarded that compared to those three relatively loose similarities, there are far more significant and irreconcilable dissimilarities between the details of Bailey's murder and behavior, and what was presented at the trial about Blaise and the assault she described in her statement and to several people. Twenty-eight irreconcilable differences between Blaise's statement and the details of Bailey's death are set forth in Tables 1 (p. 17) and 2 (p. 19). Those dissimilarities are in addition to the fourteen differences between Bailey's conduct, the crime scene and evidence, and Blaise, that are detailed in Table 4 (p. 60).

Of course, Kephart's argument also disregarded the thirteen alibi witnesses who saw or talked with Blaise in Panaca or saw her car unmoved on July 8 from shortly after midnight until after Bailey's body was discovered that evening. (See Table 3, p. 57.) The times those eyewitnesses saw Blaise and her car in Panaca encompasses the entire time of ME Simms' estimates of Bailey's time of death.

Kephart's jury argument was also misleading because it disregarded that the small degree of similarity between Bailey's murder and the event Blaise related in her statement and that she described to Dixie can innocently be explained as coincidental, because it is common for events or observances to seem on some level to be similar (or even the same). The professor authors of *Coincidences, Chaos, and All That Math Jazz*, write, "Coincidences are our constant companions in our everyday lives." (1) People think of them as being unusual, when in fact "amazing coincidences *do* happen by random chance alone." (21) The authors also note that "Coincidences surprise us because our intuition about the likelihood of an event is often wildly inaccurate." (5) Aptly for Blaise's prosecution in Las Vegas, they illustrate that point by using the example of people suckered into gambling at a Vegas casino:

> *Obviously* ... Colored lights dance from spinning disco balls while sequined servers jiggle through the crowds plying the players with cash-loosening cocktails. All this glitter sets the tone at the Big Wheel Casino in Las Vegas. Mounted on center stage, the giant wheel of fortune clicks in its characteristic rhythm and then slows to land in one of the 360 numbered slots – one for every degree of a circle. You place your bet, then 45 guests take one spin each in turn. If two spins coincidentally land in exactly the same slot, the casino wins – 360 slots, only 45 chances to make a match. You bet the farm.

> *Surprise* ... You lose your shirt. In fact, the incredible coincidence of a match will occur more than 94% of the time. *Amazing coincidences happen surprisingly often.*" (3) (emphasis added)

(Continued on page 67.)

(Continued from page 66.)

The authors emphasize that if the effort is made to do so, there is a high mathematical probability that the appearance of a coincidence can be created between any two people or events fitting into a general category.

To illustrate how that is done, the authors analyze the often-cited example of the "amazing" number of coincidences between assassinated Presidents Abraham Lincoln and John F. Kennedy. They show that the matching points between the life, career and assassination of the two men are cherry-picked facts from the pool of total information that overwhelmingly shows dissimilarities between the life of each man. (5-7)

Similarly, it was only by focusing on "cherry-picked" quasi-similarities between Bailey's murder and the attempted rape of Blaise, that Kephart was able to argue that the events were too coincidental to be different incidents. Thus when the jurors retired to consider their verdict, they were unaware that similarities are likely to exist "by random chance alone" between any two completely unrelated "sex" type crimes. An exposed penis is present in 100% of attempted rapes in which a man has pulled his pants down; a sharp object is commonly involved in an attempted rape – either brandished as a weapon by the perpetrator or used defensively by the victim; and it is common for a black man to be involved in a Las Vegas attempted rape. (Blacks comprised more than 10% of Las Vegas' population in 2001.) In addition to misleading the jurors about the importance of those details, Kephart also misdirected the jurors attention away from the dozens of irreconcilable differences between Bailey's murder and the assault on Blaise, increasing the likelihood that they could be induced to consider the events to be one and the same.

Jury's verdict

After Kephart's fire-breathing evangelical closing, some trial observers might have been concerned the jury would rush out like a lynch mob and convict Blaise in short order while in a fevered state of mind. The jury began deliberating at 6:45 p.m. on Thursday, October 5, and when they requested to go home at midnight, it was known that at least one juror wanted to at least consider the evidence. The jury resumed deliberating at 8:30 a.m. on Friday, the day before the beginning of the Columbus Day holiday weekend. In mid-afternoon, after more than ten hours of deliberation, they notified the bailiff they had reached a verdict.

The jury convicted Blaise of voluntary manslaughter with a deadly weapon and sexual penetration of a dead human body. Schieck moved for continuation of Blaise's release on $500,000 bond. Kephart opposed it, arguing she was a flight risk because she hadn't personally put up the bond money. Vega adopted Kephart's position and Blaise was taken into custody.

After the verdict, both Kephart and Schieck publicly expressed the opinion that it was a compromise: some jurors wanted to acquit Blaise, and others wanted to convict her of first or second degree murder. [226] But on the eve of a holiday weekend, the jurors settled in the middle rather than continue deliberating through the holiday, and possibly even then be unable to reach a unanimous non-compromise verdict.

Judge Vega went along with the recommendation of her former colleagues in the Clark County DA's office when on February 2, 2007, she sentenced Blaise to four to ten years for voluntary manslaughter, five to fifteen years for sexual penetration of a dead human body, and four to ten years for the use of a deadly weapon enhancement. All the sentences were ordered to be served consecutively, so they total a minimum of 13 years and a maximum of 35 years in prison. Vega ordered those lengthy prison sentences even though

Blaise was eligible for probation, she received a positive post-trial psycho-sexual evaluation from both a prosecution and a defense expert that she is a low risk to commit a sexual offense, and there was no evidence presented during the sentencing hearing that she poses any danger to the community.

Possible juror misconduct exposed after the verdict

On November 9, 2006, Hans Sherrer, publisher of *Justice:Denied* magazine, mailed a notarized affidavit to David Schieck, Blaise's lead lawyer, concerning a conversation he overheard between two jurors during Blaise's retrial. The affidavit documents that a week before jury deliberations began on October 5, 2006, jurors were discussing the case and appear to have formed opinions without consideration of the defense's case, the presentation of which began only hours before the events related in the affidavit. Schieck did not take any action related to the possible prejudicial effect of the juror's misconduct on the legality of their guilty verdicts against Blaise. The affidavit follows:

AFFIDAVIT OF HANS SHERRER

State of Washington)
) SS:
County of King   )

I, Hans Sherrer, first duly sworn, depose and say that the foregoing is true and correct to the best of my knowledge and belief:

1) On Friday, September 29, 2006, I was a spectator at the trial of Kirstin Blaise Lobato in the courtroom of Judge Valorie Vega on the 16th floor of the Clark County Courthouse in Las Vegas, Nevada.

2) At about 1 p.m. that afternoon the prosecution rested its case in chief and the defense began presenting its case.

3) At about 3:30 p.m., during the trial's afternoon "stretch" break, I was in the men's public bathroom on the 16th floor.

4) My attention was drawn to two men in the bathroom, when one referred to "differences of opinion."

5) The other man responded to the first man's comment by saying, "Deliberations are going to take a long time."

6) I noticed that both men were jurors in the Kirstin Lobato trial.

7) I recognized the man who made the response about "deliberations" was the same juror I had observed dozing (or actually sleeping) in the courtroom for about fifteen minutes on the afternoon of Tuesday, September 26, 2006, during the testimony out of turn by defense witness Dr. Michael Laufer.

8) In regards to the September 26 incident involving that juror, on the morning of Wednesday, September 27, 2006, I informed Clark County Deputy District Attorney William Kephart that I had something I wanted to jointly inform the prosecution and defense attorneys about, and later that morning I jointly informed them what I had observed the juror doing, and showed Mr. Kephart the written note I had made about the incident the preceding day at the time of the incident.

9) Based on the comments of the two jurors on the afternoon of September 29, 2006, I had reason to believe that after complete presentation of the prosecution's case, but after only partial presentation of the defense's case, the jurors were deeply divided in their opinion about the impact of the evidence presented as it affected Ms. Lobato's conviction or acquittal.

10) After Ms. Lobato's conviction on the afternoon of October 6, 2006, I read an article on Court TV's website about the trial's outcome, and that story included the analysis by both Ms. Lobato's attorney David

Schieck and Deputy DA Kephart that the verdict was a "compromise" by jurors divided between wanting to acquit her, and wanting to convict her of more than voluntary manslaughter.

11) After reading the news reports about the verdict, I knew that the jurors' conversation concerning the differing opinions formed by the jurors that I overhead in the bathroom six days before the jury began deliberating accurately reflected that the jurors were sharply divided about the case, and that they had resolved being a "hung jury" by settling on what both the defense and prosecution attorneys recognize was a compromise verdict.

12) While attending the trial I witnessed that prior to an adjournment for lunch, a "stretch break," or after a day's proceedings, Judge Vega admonished the jury with words to the effect that jurors were not to talk amongst themselves about the trial or form or express any opinion on any subject related to the trial until the case was submitted to them.

13) On the morning of October 9, 2006, the Monday after the Friday afternoon verdict in Ms. Lobato's case, I called the office of the Clark County Special Public Defender and asked for Mr. Schieck, whereupon the woman answering the telephone informed me that he was in Carson City, Nevada, and would return the following day.

14) On Tuesday, October 10, 2006, at about 10 a.m., I called the office of the Clark County Special Public Defender and asked for Mr. Schieck, whereupon the woman answering the telephone informed me he wasn't available but I could leave a message on his voice mail.

15) After being transferred to Mr. Schieck's voice mail, I left a message that I had information concerning juror conduct during Ms. Lobato's case, and that I would be sending him an affidavit.

BY: _____

Hans Sherrer

Subscribed and sworn to before me, this 9th day of November, 2006.

VII
The Jury Didn't Know That Bailey's Estimated Time of Death Excludes Blaise

The jury wasn't presented with any testimony analyzing how Medical Examiner Simms' estimates of Bailey's time of death related to the probability of whether Blaise could seriously be considered as a suspect in his death, much less prosecuted and convicted for murdering him and sexually assaulting his corpse.

Blaise unequivocally asserted in her statement that she was sexually assaulted in the dead of night, and Dixie Tienken stated that Blaise told her it was "dark" when she was attacked,[227] and Michelle Austria testified that she thought it was "nighttime" from her conversation with Blaise. [228] The prosecution didn't challenge that the incident Blaise was involved in occurred at night, so it was integral to the prosecution's theory of the crime that Blaise murdered Bailey prior to dawn. Consequently, if Bailey died after dawn, then Blaise was referring to a different incident in her statement and her conversations with people.

Simms' two estimated times of Bailey's death

Simms estimated that to a "medical certainty" it is "more than likely" that Bailey died between 12 and 18 hours from the time his body was examined at the crime scene by the coroner's examiner at 3:50 a.m. on July 9. [229] Based on that estimate Bailey died between 9:50 a.m. and 3:50 p.m. on July 8.

Simms also estimated there is a 5% "possibility" that Bailey died during the wider range of 8 to 24 hours from the time his body was examined by the coroner's examiner at 3:50 a.m.. [230] That means there was a 5% total probability that Bailey died between either 9:50 a.m. and 3:50 a.m., or 3:50 p.m. and 7:50 p.m. The entire range of Simms' estimated "possible" time of Bailey's death was that it occurred between 3:50 a.m. and 7:50 p.m. on July 8.

Based on Simms' estimate and Blaise's statement that it was dark when she was assaulted, [231] the prosecution's "theory of the crime" allows for Bailey to be murdered sometime between 3:50 a.m. and first light, which was at 4:24 a.m. on July 8. [232] The prosecution's theory of the crime allows for Bailey's death during that 34-minute window of time. [233]

Driving time from Las Vegas to Panaca

Phil Boucher, a Lincoln County based supervisor with the Nevada Department of Transportation, testified that the 171 mile trip between Panaca and Las Vegas[234] takes about three hours when traveling at an average of "72 m.p.h." on the open road. [235] He also testified that he had made the trip many times, and that the drive includes several stretches of road where a driver has to slow down considerably. Thowsen testified that when he drove up to Panaca to arrest Blaise the return trip took about 2-1/2 hours, [236] which means that based on Boucher's testimony Thowsen averaged over 85 m.p.h. on the open stretches of road. [237] During Boucher's cross-examination Kephart suggested the trip could be made in two hours, to which Boucher agreed it was "possible." However, based on the trial testimony a person would have to drive at an average of over 105 mph on the open stretches of road to make the trip in two hours. [238]

It is unknown how fast Blaise normally drove from Las Vegas to Panaca (and vice-a-versa), but there was testimony from several people that Blaise's 17-year-old car had mechanical problems. Her car actually broke down in May 2001 when she was driving to Las Vegas, after spending two weeks in Panaca around Mother's Day. [239] Furthermore, all the testimony during Blaise's trial was her car wasn't driven from the time she parked it on July 2 until it was towed by the police on July 20. That is consistent with her dad's testimony that her Fiero had mechanical problems, and that Doug Twining drove to Panaca to pick her up on July 9. So it may have been unlikely that when Blaise did drive between Las Vegas and Panaca, that she made the trip in the 2-1/2 hours that it took Thowsen, and it may even have taken her longer than Boucher's three hours. [240]

Simms' estimate of Bailey's "possible" time of death excludes Blaise

For the sake of argument, if Thowsen's driving time of 2-1/2 hours is accepted as how fast Blaise could make the trip each way from Las Vegas and Panaca, and only 30 minutes is allowed for negotiating a drug deal with Bailey, murdering him, mutilating him after his death, getting gas, going to a friend's house 15 minutes away in east Vegas to get cleaned up, disposing of her clothing, etc., the round-trip would take 5-1/2 hours. [241]

Simms' most remote "possible" time of Bailey's death was 3:50 a.m. To make the minimum 5-1/2 hour round-trip Blaise would have had to leave Panaca about 1:05 a.m., and she wouldn't have returned until about 6:35 a.m. (Although, given the 34-minute window it could have been as late as 7:09 a.m.)

Larry Lobato testified he saw and talked with Blaise when he came home from work between midnight and 1 a.m. on Sunday the 8th, and he saw her sleeping on the futon in the living room when he went to bed at 2 a.m. after watching television for a while. He also testified that was his typical routine on the nights he worked. Becky Lobato testified that when she got up to get ready for work at 5:45 a.m. she saw Blaise sleeping on the futon, and she saw her still sleeping when she left at 6:50 a.m. Likewise, that was her normal morning routine on her workdays. [242]

There was only a 3 hour and 45 minute period of time that Blaise's presence in Panaca wasn't accounted for during the early morning hours of July 8. (2 a.m. to 5:45 a.m.) That is nearly two hours less than she would have needed to make the round-trip drive to Las Vegas. Consistent with that lack of time to commit the crime, is that the prosecution's case was predicated on their assumption that Blaise solely drove to Las Vegas to obtain methamphetamines to satisfy what they claimed was her intense craving for the drug. Yet she was not only seen sleeping that morning by Becky, but John Kraft saw Blaise at 7 a.m. when he went to the Lobato house to talk with Larry and she sleepily answered the door. Larry also saw Blaise was sleepy when she woke him up to talk with Kraft, and he saw Blaise lying on the futon after he finished talking with Kraft for 10 to 15 minutes. (See Table 3, p. 57.)

Thus, based on the testimony of Larry and Becky it was physically impossible that Blaise could have been in Las Vegas at 3:50 a.m. on July 8, and Larry, Becky and Kraft's testimony about her sleeping or being sleepy supported that she hadn't taken methamphetamines that morning. That testimony is particularly compelling because Blaise related in her statement about being "out of my mind" while awake for days when she took methamphetamines. To diffuse the alibi testimony of Larry, Becky and Kraft the prosecution inferred that they lied to help Blaise, by emphasizing their relationship to her. [243] (Kraft by marriage to Blaise's aunt Shane Kraft.) If the prosecution's claim had any merit the three witnesses would have been charged with perjury – but they weren't. Furthermore, the prosecution's strategy ignored that not a single neighbor, friend, acquaintance or relative who testified as a prosecution or defense witness reported that Blaise exhibited any methamphetamine related or otherwise unusual behavior at any time on July 8. (See Table 3, p. 57.) The testimony of the eight other people who saw or talked with Blaise in Panaca on July 8 is thus consistent with the testimony of Becky that Blaise was sleeping between 5:45 a.m. and 6:50 a.m., the testimony of Larry that she was sleeping at 2 a.m., and the testimony of Larry and Kraft that she was sleepy when awakened at 7 a.m.

The testimony of the eleven people who saw or talked with Blaise on July 8 undermines the prosecution's "theory" that Blaise obtained methamphetamines that morning from Bailey – a man not known to use, sell, trade, or have methamphetamines, and none was found either in his bloodstream or at the crime scene. So there is no basis in reality for the prosecution's allegation that Blaise in Panaca – or anyone in Las Vegas – would even consider seeking to obtain methamphetamines from Bailey, much less actually do so.

As for Simms' earliest possible time of Bailey's death – 7:50 p.m. – at least seven people saw or talked with Blaise in Panaca during the 2-3/4 hours before and after that time, and Doug Twining talked with her on the telephone. (See Table 3, p. 57.) Consequently, the likelihood that Blaise could have murdered Bailey during the evening of July 8 is so outside the realm of possibility that prosecutors Kephart and DiGiacomo never even suggested it during Blaise's retrial. They exclusively focused on their assumption that Bailey was murdered during the early morning of July 8. [244]

Simms' estimate of Bailey's time of death to a "medical certainty" excludes Blaise

For the sake of argument, if Bailey was killed at 9:50 a.m., Simms' most remote estimate to a "medical certainty," and if Blaise could have driven from Las Vegas to Panaca in 2-1/2 hours, and if she only took 30 minutes to mutilate Bailey after his death, dispose of her clothes, get gas, clean-up at her friend's house 15 minutes away in east Vegas, etc, then the earliest she could have returned to Panaca would have been about 12:50 p.m. Yet that is more than an hour after three eyewitnesses – who were not relatives of Blaise and who the prosecution didn't even suggest were lying – testified that they positively saw her between 11 and 11:30 a.m. in Panaca on July 8. (See Table 3, p. 57.) Those three people saw Blaise independent of one another, and one of them, her neighbor Michelle Austria, testified that she went four-wheeling with Blaise at 11:30 a.m.

Even if Blaise could have averaged well over 100 m.p.h. and made the trip in two hours, she still would have arrived in Panaca after noon, which is more than half-an-hour after the time that the three witnesses either saw her or were four-wheeling with her.

As for Simms' earliest estimated time of Bailey's death to a "medical certainty" – 3:50 p.m. – Blaise would have had to leave Panaca about 1 p.m. and the earliest she could have returned was about 6:35 p.m. Yet one person saw her in Panaca at about 1 p.m., three people saw or talked with her between 4 p.m. and 4:30 p.m., another person talked with her for 30 to 45 minutes between 5 and 6 p.m., and a different person talked with her around 6 p.m. (See Table 3, p. 57.) Consequently, the likelihood that Blaise could have murdered Bailey in Las Vegas during the mid-afternoon of July 8 is so outside the realm of possibility that prosecutors Kephart and DiGiacomo never even suggested it during Blaise's retrial. Instead they ignored Simms' estimate of Bailey's time of death to a "medical certainty" and exclusively focused on Simms' most remote "possible" estimate that he could have died at 3:50 a.m., prior to dawn on July 8.

Yet curiously, during his closing argument Schieck did not explain to the jury the incontrovertible conclusion that based on Simms' estimate of Bailey's time of death to a "medical certainty," it is as outside the realm of possibility that Blaise could have killed Bailey in Las Vegas, as it is if he had instead been murdered across the Atlantic Ocean in London – i.e., it is zero. It is not possible Blaise that could have murdered Bailey between 9:50 a.m. and 3:50 p.m.

Simms testified during Blaise's retrial that the range of his estimate of Bailey's time of death could be plotted as a bell curve. So what Schieck did do during his closing argument was display to the jury a hand-drawn "bell curve" of Simms' estimate that to a "medical certainty" Bailey died between 9:50 am and 3:50 p.m. Schieck suggested that Bailey's death most likely occurred in the middle range of the curve – 12:50 p.m. – but he didn't explain what that means. [245] Furthermore, Schieck didn't present a person skilled in mathematics as a defense expert witness to provide an authoritative explanation of how "bell curve" analysis relates to Simms' two estimates of Bailey's time of death: His estimate to a "medical certainty" and his estimated "possible" time of death.

A bell curve is a visualization of an event's mathematical probability

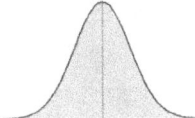 The "bell curve" (also known as a "normal curve") was first identified more than 250 years ago by French mathematician Abraham de Moivre as a way to visually plot the probability of an event's occurrence based on a set of criteria.[246] A "bell curve" is commonly associated with population and mortality analysis, but it has application to estimating the probability of a wide range of activities. For example, based on a javelin thrower's past performances, a "bell curve" can be used to visually plot the probability of how far he or she will throw the javelin in an upcoming competition.[247]

Moivre intuitively recognized, and it has been verified through centuries of practical application, that the probability of an event's occurrence is heavily weighted toward the center of a "bell curve" – and it very rapidly decreases toward both end points. (See the percentages plotted on the "bell curve" in Figure 1, p. 82.)

Probability theory is an important branch of mathematics that is relied on in the engineering of critical products from the space shuttle to nuclear power plants, to designing international telephone systems, to evaluating the safety of vaccines.[248] The accuracy of a "bell curve" to plot an event's probability has been demonstrated to the point that it has "become both a cultural icon and an important mathematical concept."[249]

Bell curve analysis of Simms' estimate of Bailey's "possible" time of death excludes Blaise

A "bell curve" analysis demonstrates that based on Simms' estimate that Bailey's "possible" time of death was between 3:50 a.m. and 7:50 p.m., there is only a 0.000000018% probability that Bailey died between 3:50 a.m. and 4:24 a.m., which is when dawn was on July 8.[250] That is the equivalent of 1 chance in 55,466,024. The minuteness of that probability is put in perspective by the fact that any person reading this has a 1 chance in 1,756 of dying in any given year from an injury caused by a fall, auto accident, etc.[251] That means the odds are more than 31,587 times greater (55,466,024/1,756) that any one of Blaise's jurors would have been expected to die of an injury from an accident in the year prior to (or after) her conviction, than that Bailey died prior to dawn.

Furthermore, the odds are 1 in 146 (1,756/12) that one of Blaise's twelve jurors would have died of an injury in the year prior to (or after) her conviction. Thus it is 379,904 times more likely (55,466,024/146) that one of the twelve jurors would have died of an injury in the year before her conviction, than that Bailey died prior to dawn. Yet we know for 100% certainty that not a single juror died of an injury in the year prior to Blaise's October 6, 2006 conviction. That none of the jurors died of an injury in the year before Blaise's conviction highlights the dramatically less likely probability that Bailey died prior to dawn – and thus it is extraordinarily improbable that Blaise could have murdered him.

Probability of when Bailey died based on his "possible" time of death on the morning of July 8			
Time range	Explanation	Probability	1 chance in x
Died between 3:50 am and 4:24 am	Dawn	0.000000018	55,466,024
Died between 3:50 am and 5:01 am	Light enough to legally turn off headlights	0.00000016	6,090,226
Died between 3:50 am and 5:30 am	Sunrise	0.00000083	1,203,272
Died between 3:50 am and 7:00 am	Time during which three alibi witnesses related to Blaise saw her in Panaca.	0.000069	14,444
Died between 3:50 am and 8:00 am	Latest time Bailey could have died so Blaise could have arrived in Panaca by 11 a.m. when three non-relative alibi witnesses saw her.	0.00079	1,257

The overwhelming probability that Bailey died during daylight is emphasized by the fact that it is mathematically more than *31 million times more likely* that Bailey died at 12:50 p.m. – the "bell curves" mid-point – than prior to dawn on July 8. [252]

If all things were equal the lack of likelihood that Bailey died prior to dawn would apply to Simms' estimate that Bailey possibly died in the early evening by 7:50 p.m.

However, in prosecuting Blaise on the basis that Bailey died prior to dawn, Kephart and DiGiacomo disregarded that all things were not equal in considering whether Bailey died at Simms' estimate of his "possible" time of death that was furthermost from (pre-dawn) or closest (evening) to when his body was examined at the crime scene. The bloody shoeprints leading away from Bailey's body were still moist when his crime scene was first observed by a law enforcement officer at 10:50 p.m. – and it is impossible for the shoeprints not to have dried if deposited in the pre-dawn hours of July 8 and then baked in the intense heat and low humidity of summer in Las Vegas, until being observed more than 18 hours later approaching midnight. [253] Additionally, all the salient crime scene, weather, and medical factors that would accelerate decomposition and rigor mortis in Bailey's body support that his time of death was as close to the time his body was discovered by Richard Shott as Simms' estimate allows. (For a complete analysis see the section, "Bailey's likely time of death," later in this Chapter.)

Even if Bailey died at 3:50 a.m., or shortly thereafter, in spite of the astronomical mathematical odds and scientific principles that undercut the possibility that was his time of death, Larry Lobato testified he saw Blaise less than two hours before then at 2 a.m., and Becky Lobato saw her less than two hours after then at 5:45 a.m. – so based on their testimony Blaise could not have been in Las Vegas. The truthfulness of the Lobato's testimony can be assessed by its consistency with the scientific, medical and mathematical evidence, other alibi witness testimony supporting their testimony that Blaise was in Panaca on July 8, and that the prosecution did not even suggest there was any factual basis to charge the Lobatos with perjury.

Conversely, if Bailey died at the earliest "possible" time of 7:50 p.m., seven people saw or talked with Blaise in Panaca during either the preceding 2-3/4 hours or the following 2-3/4 hours, during which she would have been traveling to and from Las Vegas, and Doug Twining talked with her on the telephone.

The "bell curve" in Figure 1 (p. 82) explains what the jury did not hear from Schieck in his closing argument: Taken at face value without any analysis, Simms' most remote "possible" time of Bailey's death may appear to "possibly" support the prosecution's contention that it is "possible" Blaise murdered Bailey prior to dawn and then immediately drove back to Panaca in her Fiero. However, when subjected to "bell curve" analysis that "possibility" is revealed as so mathematically improbable that in the absence of compelling and irrefutable science based evidence to the contrary, by itself that analysis removes Blaise from consideration as Bailey's murderer.

Bell curve analysis of Simms' estimate of Bailey's time of death to a "medical certainty" excludes Blaise

Simms' estimate of Bailey's time of death to a "medical certainty" solely encompasses the daylight hours from mid-morning (9:50 a.m.) to mid-afternoon (3:50 p.m.).

A "bell curve" analysis demonstrates that based on Simms' estimate there is a 99.74% (9,974 out of 10,000) probability that Bailey died between 10:35 a.m. and 3:05 p.m. (See Figure 2, p. 82.) There is only a .13% probability that Bailey died between either 9:50 a.m. and 10:35 a.m. or 3:05 p.m. and 3:50 p.m.

However, if in spite of the astronomical odds against it, Bailey was killed at the most remote time to a "medical certainty" of 9:50 a.m., Blaise is excluded as his murderer because five people saw or talked with her during either the preceding 2-3/4 hours or the following 2-3/4 hours, and next door neighbors saw her car parked in front of her parents house. (See Table 3, p. 57.)

Conversely, if Bailey died at the earliest time of 3:50 p.m., six people saw or talked with her during either the preceding 2-3/4 hours or the following 2-3/4 hours. (See Table 3, p. 57.)

As explained previously, the evidence of Blaise's presence in Panaca during the mid-morning and afternoon of July 8 was so overwhelming that the prosecution didn't even attempt to argue that Bailey died during the range of Simms' estimate to a "medical certainty."

Bell curve analysis supports that Bailey died during daylight hours

The prosecution's case against Blaise rested on the assumption that Bailey was murdered during the pre-dawn hours of July 8. That resulted in the prosecution's focus on Simms' estimate that it is "possible" he died as remotely as 3:50 a.m. (when it was dark), while Schieck focused on Simms' estimate to a "medical certainty" that he died between 9:50 a.m. and 3:50 p.m. (when it was daylight).

Undermining the prosecution's assumption of when Bailey, is that based on Simms' estimated "possible" time of his death, "bell curve" analysis establishes there is a 0.000000018% probability that Bailey died between 3:50 a.m. and dawn at 4:24 a.m. [254] (See Figure 1, p. 82.) Even stretching the time to 5:01 a.m., which was when it was so light that it was legal to operate a vehicle without headlights, the probability is still only 0.00000016% (1 chance in 6,167,630) that Bailey died during that 1 hour and 11 minute period of time between 3:50 a.m. to 5:01 a.m.. [255]

In contrast, there is a 99.9999982% probability that Bailey died during the hours between 4:24 a.m. in the early morning and 7:50 p.m. in the early evening, based on Simms' estimate of Bailey's "possible" time of death. (See Figure 1, p. 82.) Again, even if the time is expanded to include when it was so light that drivers could legally drive without headlights, the probability is still 99.999984% that Bailey died between 5:01 a.m. and 7:50 p.m.

Furthermore, there is a 100% probability – or absolute certainty – that Bailey died during daylight, based on Simms' estimate to a medical certainty" that Bailey's death occurred between 9:50 a.m. and 3:50 p.m. (4 hours 20 minutes after sunrise and 4 hours 10 minutes before sunset, respectively.)

Bailey's likely time of death

Bailey's likely time of death can be estimated from analyzing the information that is known:

• The bloody shoeprints leading away from Bailey's body were moist when the police arrived on the scene beginning at 10:50 p.m.

• The trash enclosure inside of which Bailey was killed and his body was found, was open on one end and on three sides it had high walls made of concrete blocks.

• Bailey's body was found lying near one of the block walls, next to a large trash bin.

• Bailey's was wearing a shirt and his body was found covered with a thick layer of loose trash (presumably from the trash bin).

• The trash covering Bailey's body was removed piece by piece, and his body wasn't fully exposed until hours after the police arrived.

- Bailey's covered body was concealed from exposure to the trash enclosure's open end by the large trash bin.
- July is Las Vegas' hottest month and it doesn't appreciably cool off after the sun goes down. [256]
- Simms testified that "ambient air temperature" is one of the most important factors affecting the rate of decomposition and the process of rigor mortis. [257]
- Simms testified that heat accelerates the decomposition and rigor mortis process. [258]
- Simms testified that concrete blocks retain the heat from sunlight and the air temperature, and they radiate heat, even after nightfall, speeding up both decomposition and the rigor mortis process. [259]
- Simms testified that the trash enclosure where Bailey's body was found would have retained heat and accelerated both his decomposition and the rigor mortis process. [260]
- Simms testified the trash covering Bailey's body would have accelerated his decomposition and the rigor mortis process by retaining his body heat. [261]
- The plastic sheeting wrapped around Bailey's body also would have contributed to retention of his body heat and the acceleration of rigor mortis and his decomposition.
- Death following physical exertion accelerates the rigor mortis process, and Bailey died after an intense struggle as indicated by his defensive wounds. [262]

Thus every salient factor related to the location and covering of Bailey's body, combined with the extreme Las Vegas heat and Bailey's physical exertion, contributed to the acceleration of his decomposition and the rigor mortis process: He was murdered in July when the heat is most extreme in Las Vegas; he was lying next to a concrete block wall that retained and radiated heat; his body was covered retaining heat; the enclosure where his body was found retained and radiated heat; and he exerted himself immediately prior to his death.

Simms testified during Blaise's retrial that Bailey was not in full rigor mortis at 3 a.m., but he was at 3:50 a.m. [263] He also testified that under *normal* conditions full rigor mortis sets in 12 to 18 hours after death. He estimated that occurred in 60% of cases, so 40% of cases involve less or more time for full rigor mortis to set in. Simms also testified that it was "possible" Bailey could have died in the range of 8 to 24 hours from the time his body was examined by the coroner's examiner.

The conditions under which Bailey's body was found was a nearly "perfect scenario" for the acceleration of his rigor mortis process to occur much faster than the normal time of 12 to 18 hours. Considering the extreme conditions of excessive summer heat, heat radiation by the block trash enclosure, retention of Bailey's body heat, and Bailey's physical exertion immediately prior to his death, any one of which would have accelerated the onset of rigor mortis, it would certainly seem reasonable to conclude that *at a minimum* Bailey's rigor mortis likely occurred at the most rapid rate allowed by Simms' estimate of his "possible" time of death. That was eight hours prior to his body's crime scene examination at 3:50 a.m., which means Bailey would have died about 7:50 p.m. A time of death close to when Bailey's body was discovered is also consistent with the shoeprints leading away from his body that were still moist when the police arrived at the crime scene.

Additional support for Bailey's death on the evening of July 8 shortly before the discovery of his body, is that when he was examined by the coroner's examiner he didn't exhibit any significant degree of decomposition – even though the conditions were nearly perfect for the accelerated decomposition of his body after death. The absence of Bailey's decomposition in identifying his time of death was specifically addressed by Simms during Blaise's preliminary hearing on August 7, 2001. He testified that when he performed Bailey's autopsy "The body wasn't manifesting any significant degree of decomposition, so *I would say he had died a lot closer to the time he was discovered than not."* [264] That was one reason that Simms estimated during that hearing that Bailey died "more likely than not some time within 12 hours of when he was discovered." [265] Simms' testimony allowed for Bailey's death to have occurred within minutes of his body's discovery by Richard Shott.

Shott gave his statement to Thowsen about three hours after he discovered Bailey's body. [266] Shott described that he went to a nearby pay phone and called 911 immediately after confirming that he had discovered a man's body in the trash enclosure. That emergency call was received at 10:36 p.m. So Shott would have first seen Bailey's body between 10:15 p.m. and 10:30 p.m. That means Bailey's most remote time of death was no later than 10:15 a.m., and his earliest time of death was immediately before Shott discovered him, or no earlier than 10:15 p.m., based on Simms' estimate during Blaise's preliminary hearing.

In light of the foregoing, it is somewhat remarkable that the prosecution's case depended on the assumption –without any corroborating scientific or medical testimony or other evidence, or even any logical argument – that full rigor mortis formed in Bailey's body at the *slowest possible rate* allowed by Simms' estimate of Bailey's "possible" time of death, which during Blaise's retrial he testified was 3:50 a.m. Yet based on Simms' testimony about rigor mortis, decomposition, the crime scene and the weather conditions, that estimate can only possibly apply to Las Vegas' coldest days in the dead of winter with the fully exposed body of a person who didn't exert him or herself – *the exact opposite* of the circumstances of Bailey's death.

There are seven eyewitnesses who place Blaise in Panaca between 6 p.m. and when Doug Twining arrived at about 1 a.m. on July 9 to drive her to Las Vegas. She also talked that evening on the telephone with Twining before he arrived. There is no question Blaise was in Panaca on Sunday evening, and the prosecution didn't even contest that fact. Consequently, based on Bailey's likely time of death during the evening of July 8 between 7:50 p.m. and 10:15-10:30 p.m., it is a physical impossibility that Blaise could have murdered him – because she was in Panaca 170 miles from Las Vegas. [267]

Reasonable doubt and probability of guilt

The degree of probability necessary to overcome reasonable doubt about a person's lack of guilt has not been established as a legal standard. However, in 1994 the U.S. Supreme Court did rule in *Victor v Nebraska*, 511 U.S. 1 (1994), that a jury instruction is acceptable that describes beyond a reasonable doubt as "a subjective state of near certitude of the guilt of the accused." (15) This "near certitude" is reflected in "the very high level of probability required by the constitution in criminal cases." (15) The Court also acknowledged the appropriateness of juror's reliance on "strong probabilities" of a defendant's guilt, but in so doing, "it emphasized the fact that those probabilities must be so strong as to exclude any reasonable doubt, and that is unquestionably the law." (22)

While the Supreme Court hasn't attached a specific figure to what the "strong" probability "of near certitude" is that it described in *Victor v. Nebraska*, a year later, in *Schlup v. Delo*, 513 U.S. 298 (1995), the Court approving cited the oft cited quote from Thomas Starkie's *Evidence* 751 (1824): "The maxim of the law is … that it is better that ninety-nine … offenders shall escape than that one innocent man be condemned." Starkie's formulation is similar to Benjamin Franklin's pronouncement "that it is better one hundred guilty Persons should escape than that one innocent Person should suffer is a maxim that has been long and generally approved." [268] Under that standard, less than a 99% probability of a defendant's guilt constitutes reasonable doubt, and he or she must be acquitted.

Another expression of the probability necessary to establish guilt is Sir John Fortescue's statement in 1470, "one would much rather that twenty guilty persons should escape the punishment of death, than that one innocent person should be condemned and suffer capitally." [269] Under that standard, less than a 95% probability of a person's guilt constitutes reasonable doubt.

Sir William Blackstone's well known admonition is it is "better that ten guilty persons escape than that one innocent suffer." [270] Similarly, in protesting the Salem witch trials Increase Mather wrote on October 3, 1692, "It were better that Ten Suspected Witches should escape, than that the Innocent Person should be Condemned." [271] Those pronouncements support a standard that less than 90% probability of guilt constitutes reasonable doubt.

Maimonides, a 12th century legal scholar, believed: "It is better and more satisfactory to acquit a thousand guilty persons than to put a single innocent one to death." [272] Under that standard, less than a 99.9% probability of a person's guilt constitutes reasonable doubt.

Thus, looking back more than 700 years, commentators consider that a standard of at least a 90% probability of guilt, and as much as 99.9%, is necessary to find that a person committed a crime.

Although there is no recognized legal standard of the probability of guilt beyond a reasonable doubt that is necessary for the prosecution to overcome a defendant's presumption of innocence, that probability obviously has to significantly exceed the preponderance of the evidence (51% probability) standard relied on to decide a civil trial. The U.S. Supreme Court made it crystal clear in *Victor v. Nebraska* (1994) that the implicit assumption in the legal standard of proof beyond a reasonable doubt is that a criminal conviction depends on a "very high level of probability" of guilt. That high probability is reflected in the commentators estimates that require a minimum 90% certainty of guilt to support a conviction, and as high as 99.9%.

Probability and evidence analysis supports reasonable doubt that Blaise murdered Bailey

Analyzing Simms' estimates, during Blaise's retrial, of Bailey's time of death by the technique of mathematical probability in concert with the trial testimony and exhibits is a realistic way to evaluate whether the prosecution met its burden of proving Blaise's guilt beyond a reasonable doubt. The following are key points summarizing how reasonable doubt about Blaise's guilt can be assessed:

• Blaise was unequivocal in her statement that she was assaulted at night, and the prosecution accepted that as true. [273] Consequently, based on Simms' estimate of Bailey's "possible" time of death, the prosecution's case against her relied on the assumption that Bailey's murder occurred during the roughly half-an-hour period between 3:50 a.m. and the onset of daylight at 4:24 a.m. Bell curve analysis reveals there is a .000000018% (1 in 55,466,024) probability that Bailey died during that period of time. [274] (See Figure 1, p. 82.) Even expanding the "possible" time of Bailey's death to when it was light enough for drivers to legally turn off their headlights (5:01 p.m.) only increases the probability to 1 chance in 6,090,226 that Bailey died between 3:50 a.m. and 5:10 a.m.

• There is no physical or forensic evidence Blaise was at the crime scene. She is excluded by DNA testing as the source of crime scene chewing gum, cigarette butts and a pubic hair; she is excluded as the source of crime scene fingerprints; bloody shoeprints leading away from Bailey's body were determined to be 2-1/2 to 3 sizes larger than her shoe size; and her car's tires didn't match the undisturbed tire tracks found next to the trash enclosure. (This exclusionary evidence is particularly significant because the prosecution's case is based on the assumption that Bailey's murder was the result of an alleged methamphetamine fueled hysterical rage by Blaise during which she would have been anything but careful about what she did, or what evidence would have been left at the crime scene.) [275]

• There is no evidence Blaise had ever met Bailey, or even knew who he was or where he lived.

- There is no eyewitness, gas receipt or gas station, convenience store, or bank surveillance video placing Blaise or her car in Las Vegas at any time on July 8 (or anytime between July 2 and July 9).

- There is no significant detail in Blaise's statement describing the sexual assault on her at the end of May that matches the details of Bailey's murder or his crime scene. [276] (See Table 1, p. 17 and Table 2, p. 19.)

- There is unrebutted alibi testimony from eleven people who saw and/or talked with Blaise (and two other people saw her parked car) in Panaca on July 8 from shortly after midnight until after Bailey's body was first observed by a policeman at 10:50 p.m. in Las Vegas.

- During the five-and-a-half years between Bailey's murder and Blaise's retrial the prosecution could not find a single person who at any time had ever seen Blaise at the Nevada State Bank where Bailey lived in the trash enclosure, or a single witness who said they had ever seen Blaise with Bailey, or anyone who had ever heard her talking about him prior to his death.

- During the five-and-a-half years between Bailey's murder and Blaise's retrial the prosecution could not find a single person who ever saw Bailey use, sell, trade, buy or possess methamphetamines – which Blaise had been known to use, but Bailey did not – yet the core of the prosecution's "theory of the crime" was that Blaise drove from Panaca to Las Vegas in her car to obtain methamphetamines from Bailey to satisfy her alleged craving.

- There was testimony that Blaise's car was unreliable, and there was testimony that her parents were aware on Saturday July 7 that she was planning to go back to Las Vegas, and in fact Doug Twining arrived in Panaca during the early morning of July 9 to take her back to Las Vegas with him.

- Testimony established that methamphetamines was readily available in Lincoln County (Panaca). So the prosecution's "theory of the crime" that Blaise drove to Las Vegas to obtain methamphetamines from Bailey ignored the logical absurdity and incongruity of why Blaise would have driven a 340 mile round-trip in an unreliable vehicle to obtain a drug that she could have obtained with no problem within minutes in or near Panaca by driving, and that may have been available within walking distance of her parent's house.

- There was no blood found in Blaise's car based on conclusive forensic tests of swabs collected from two spots that presumptive tests indicated might have the presence of iron. (Although blood has iron in it, so do many natural and artificial sources that could leave an iron deposit detected by a presumptive test – and that is later conclusively disproven as blood.)

- There was no blood or any human biological matter found on Blaise's baseball bat that she kept in her car for self-defense.

- None of Bailey's blood or biological matter was found on the black shoes that Blaise specifically identified in her statement she was wearing when she was assaulted. (See Table 2, p. 19.)

- The prosecution ignored Simms' estimate of Bailey's time of death to a "medical certainty," because it solely encompassed daylight hours and absolutely excludes Blaise from consideration as Bailey's murderer.

- Blaise's prosecution was based on a cherry-picked time of death for Bailey that ignored not only Simms' estimate of his time of death to a "medical certainty" – but that also ignored the 96.5% of Simms' estimate of Bailey's "possible" time of death that fell after dawn – 4:24 a.m. to 7:50 p.m. [277]

- The prosecution did not contest the reliability of Blaise's alibi witnesses positively establishing that numerous people saw or talked with her in Panaca from 11 a.m. until after Bailey's body was discovered about 10:15 p.m. (Three other witnesses saw and/or talked with Blaise between about 12:30 a.m. and 7:15 a.m.)

- Blaise was assaulted in the dead of night, so the extraordinarily high probability of more than 99.99% that Bailey died after dawn on July 8 [278] is consistent with the defense's contention that his murder and the assault on Blaise were two different events. That they were separate events logically and directly explains why the crime scene evidence, forensic tests, circumstantial evidence and alibi testimony excludes Blaise from any connection to Bailey's murder: A person not present at a crime scene is not going to leave any evidence or have any evidence in her possession linking her to a crime she did not commit.

• The absence of incriminating evidence is buttressed by the lack of any details in Blaise's statement identifying the attempted rape of her in Las Vegas was the same event as Bailey's brutal murder.

A mathematician could calculate the probability that a person could be Bailey's murderer given the above facts. While that probability is not known, what is known is that it would be significantly less than the more than 99.999% probability that Bailey died after dawn on July 8.

If Bailey didn't die when it was dark, then on its face his murder and the attempted rape of Blaise were two different events. That doesn't even consider her alibi witnesses and other evidence that reduces the probability even more that she could have been present at the crime scene – which is a predicate to proving the prosecution's allegation that she, and she alone murdered Bailey. The former has to be proven before the latter can even be considered as a possibility.

The proof beyond a reasonable doubt necessary to overcome the presumption of absolute innocence cloaking a defendant is a subjective evaluation based on each jurors knowledge, prejudices, life experience, outside influences, and consideration of the evidence. Regardless of a juror's decision making process, numerous legal commentators over a period of centuries consider that being convinced of guilt to a certainty of 90% or more is necessary to convict a defendant.

Overall, the probability that Blaise could be Bailey's murderer based on the assumption he died prior to dawn on July 8 is significantly less than 1/10,000th of 1%. That is more than 900,000 times less than the degree of certainty required by a minimal reasonable doubt standard of 90% certainty about an accused person's guilt. (Keep in mind that no matter how low the probability is that Blaise could have been present at the crime scene, that probability depends on the assumption that Blaise's three alibi witnesses lied about seeing her on Panaca on the early morning of July 8. If it is assumed they were telling the truth then the probability is zero that Blaise was either in Las Vegas or murdered Bailey – and there is 100% certainty that she is actually and factually innocent of the crime.)

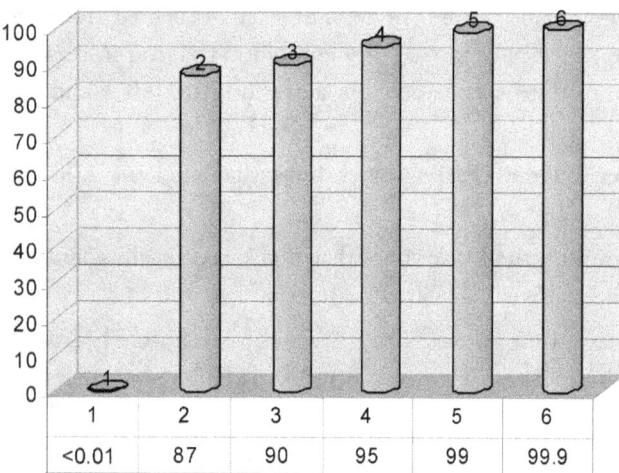

Probability Bailey died prior to dawn contrasted with certainty of guilt percentages considered necessary to find a defendant guilty

1	2	3	4	5	6
<0.01	87	90	95	99	99.9

1 <0.01% Probability that Bailey died prior to dawn
2 87% Surveys of laypersons
3 90% Blackstone & Mather
4 95% Fortescue
5 99% Franklin & Starkie
6 99.9% Maimonides

On its face, the probability that Bailey was murdered during the only period of time in which Blaise "possibly" could have committed the crime is so far below the prosecution's required burden of proof that it doesn't even have a pretence of supporting her conviction by the legal standard of proof beyond a reasonable doubt.

The much less than 1% probability that Blaise was present at the crime scene (i.e., it is significantly *more than* a 99% probability she is factually innocent) excludes her from any consideration as Bailey's murderer based on centuries of estimates of the certainty of guilt necessary to support a conviction. In fact, because the probability of Blaise's guilt is quantifiable by "bell curve" analysis as much less than 1%, she is excluded as Bailey's murderer even if a person believes the radical un-American notion that it is better that 99 innocent people be convicted than one guilty person go free. (i.e., a 99% probability of innocence is insufficient for acquittal.)

Blaise's jury wasn't informed that Bailey's "possible" time of death excludes her

Somewhat inexplicably, Schieck didn't explain to the jury during his closing argument through argument and visual aids, such as a Power Point presentation, why Blaise is excluded from consideration as a suspect by Simms' estimate of Bailey's "possible" time of death that encompassed a short period of time prior to dawn.

Schieck did use a hand-drawn "bell curve" when arguing to the jury that Simms' estimate to a "medical certainty" – that Bailey died between 9:50 a.m. and 3:50 p.m. – excluded Blaise. It is odd, however, that he used it at that time because the prosecution didn't contend that Bailey was murdered during daylight, and there is absolute certainty that Blaise could not have murdered Bailey during the time of Simms' estimate to a "medical certainty."

"Bell curve" probability analysis completely undermines the prosecution's contention that Bailey was murdered at the most remote end of Simms' estimate of his "possible" time of death. That means there is a miniscule probability substantially less than 1% (less than .000000018%) that Blaise could have murdered Bailey as the prosecution argued prior to dawn on July 8 – and that is without even considering the exclusionary alibi testimony of Larry and Becky Lobato and John Kraft, the exclusionary crime scene evidence, and many other factors that make Blaise's "possible" involvement in Bailey's murder move from being highly improbable, into the realm of being impossible.

The magnitude of the error in pursuing Blaise's prosecution is highlighted by the analysis showing that Bailey's time of death was in all probability between 7:50 p.m. and 10:15 p.m. on July 8, when it is indisputable that Blaise was in Panaca. The jurors lack of knowing that Simms' estimates of Bailey's time of death exculpates Blaise, had a dramatic effect on their verdict – in both of her trials. They did not, and could not have made an informed decision in convicting her because they were unaware of the infinitesimally small probability that Blaise could have been in Las Vegas at the time of Bailey's death.

One detail about Bailey's murder that is known with absolute certainty is that at the time of his death his murderer or murderers were in Las Vegas – not 170 miles away in Panaca which is where the evidence establishes Blaise was when he was fatally assaulted.

Figure 1

Bell curve probabilities that Bailey died within a period of time based on his time of death estimated by ME Simms during Blaise's retrial.

It is "possible" that Duran Bailey died between 3:50 a.m. and 7:50 p.m., July 8, 2001 *

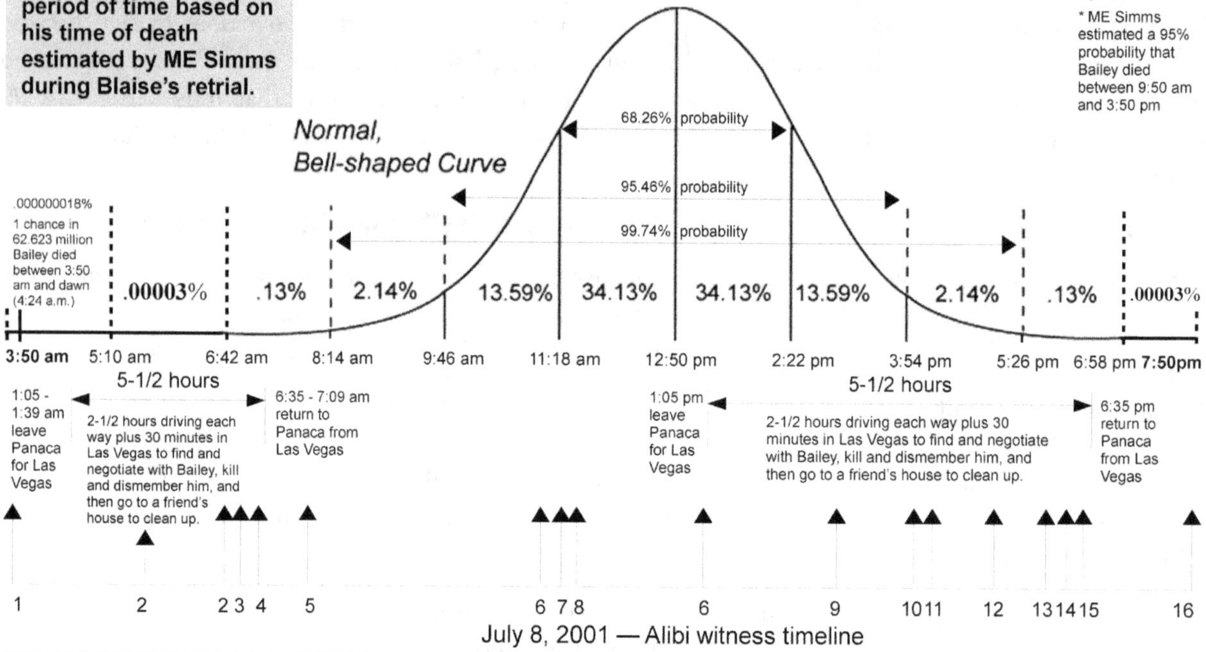

* ME Simms estimated a 95% probability that Bailey died between 9:50 am and 3:50 pm

Normal, Bell-shaped Curve

68.26% probability
95.46% probability
99.74% probability

.000000018% 1 chance in 62.623 million Bailey died between 3:50 am and dawn (4:24 a.m.)

.00003% .13% 2.14% 13.59% 34.13% 34.13% 13.59% 2.14% .13% .00003%

3:50 am | 5:10 am | 6:42 am | 8:14 am | 9:46 am | 11:18 am | 12:50 pm | 2:22 pm | 3:54 pm | 5:26 pm | 6:58 pm 7:50pm

5-1/2 hours | 5-1/2 hours

1:05 - 1:39 am leave Panaca for Las Vegas

2-1/2 hours driving each way plus 30 minutes in Las Vegas to find and negotiate with Bailey, kill and dismember him, and then go to a friend's house to clean up.

6:35 - 7:09 am return to Panaca from Las Vegas

1:05 pm leave Panaca for Las Vegas

2-1/2 hours driving each way plus 30 minutes in Las Vegas to find and negotiate with Bailey, kill and dismember him, and then go to a friend's house to clean up.

6:35 pm return to Panaca from Las Vegas

1   2   3 4 5   6 7 8   6   9   10 11   12   13 14 15   16

July 8, 2001 — Alibi witness timeline

Alibi witnesses for Blaise's presence in Panaca on July 8, 2001

1	Larry Lobato	Midnight - 2 am	7	Michelle Austria	11:30 am	13	Shane Kraft	6 - 8 pm
2	Becky Lobato	5:45 - 6:50 am	8	Clint Holman	11:30 am	14	Becky Lobato	Evening - 1 am
3	John Kraft	7 am	9	Ashley Lobato	3 - 4 pm	15	Ashley Lobato	Evening - 12:20 am
4	Larry Lobato	7 - 7:15 am	10	Chris Carrington	4 - 6:45 pm	16	John Kraft	8 pm
5	Robert McCrosky	Morning	11	Becky Lobato	4:20 pm	17	Chris Carrington	10 pm
6	Jo Ann Dennert	11 am - 1 pm	12	Kendre Thunstrom	5 - 6 pm			

Witnesses name, timeline identifying number, and time they saw or talked with Blaise.

Figure 2

"Medical certainty" that Duran Bailey died between 9:50 a.m. and 3:50 p.m., July 8, 2001

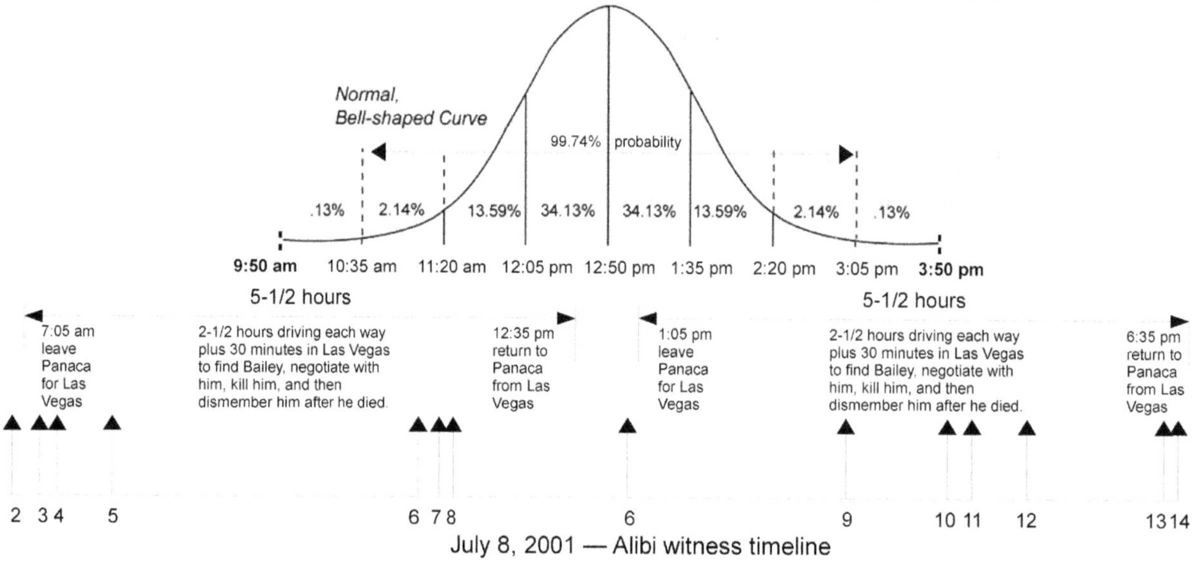

Normal, Bell-shaped Curve

99.74% probability

.13% 2.14% 13.59% 34.13% 34.13% 13.59% 2.14% .13%

9:50 am | 10:35 am | 11:20 am | 12:05 pm | 12:50 pm | 1:35 pm | 2:20 pm | 3:05 pm | 3:50 pm

5-1/2 hours | 5-1/2 hours

7:05 am leave Panaca for Las Vegas

2-1/2 hours driving each way plus 30 minutes in Las Vegas to find Bailey, negotiate with him, kill him, and then dismember him after he died.

12:35 pm return to Panaca from Las Vegas

1:05 pm leave Panaca for Las Vegas

2-1/2 hours driving each way plus 30 minutes in Las Vegas to find Bailey, negotiate with him, kill him, and then dismember him after he died.

6:35 pm return to Panaca from Las Vegas

2   3 4   5   6 7 8   6   9   10 11   12   13 14

July 8, 2001 — Alibi witness timeline

VIII
Postscript

More than six years after Duran Bailey's murder and mutilation all the physical and forensic evidence, and expert evaluation of the crime scene and the nature of the crime, points to one or more males as the perpetrator. Yet Blaise has twice been convicted in this death without any evidence she was within 170 miles of Las Vegas at any time on the day of his murder.

No person saw her in Las Vegas on July 3 through July 8. No person saw her car in Las Vegas during that period of time. She didn't say in her statement that she was in Las Vegas on any of those days. No person saw her leave Panaca for Las Vegas during that period of time, and no person says she talked to him or her from Las Vegas on any of those days. Furthermore, there is no gas receipt or any credit card receipt, nor any bank, casino, gas station or convenience store surveillance video showing that she was outside of Lincoln County at any time on July 3 through July 8.

If Blaise was in Panaca 170 miles from Las Vegas on July 8, then it is a physical impossibility for her to have murdered Bailey. That she was in Panaca is the most logical, and the most direct explanation for why there is no evidence whatsoever found in Blaise's possession, in her car, on Bailey's body, or at the crime scene linking her to Bailey's' murder – or that supports she ever met him or even knew who he was.

The absence of any evidence that Blaise was in Las Vegas on the day of Bailey's murder, and the absence of any physical or forensic evidence linking her to Bailey's murder, is consistent with the absence of details in Dixie Tienken's recollection of her conversation with Blaise that identifies Blaise was referring to Bailey's murder when she described being sexually assaulted at night in Las Vegas. Likewise, Laura Johnson's double hearsay testimony of what Tienken told her that Blaise said about the assault is inconsistent with the very peculiar details of Bailey's murder. Neither is there any detail in Blaise's statement suggesting that the attempted rape of her in a Las Vegas hotel parking lot and Bailey's murder were anything other than different events, at different times, at different locations, on different days, involving different persons and very different injuries.

Consistent with the absence of evidence linking Blaise to Bailey's murder is that based on the testimony of the prosecution's medical expert, M.E. Simms, there is the overwhelming probability that Bailey died during daylight hours. That time of death conclusively identifies his murder as a different event than the assault on Blaise that occurred at night after midnight. Also supporting that they were separate events is the detailed analysis in Section VI that identifies Bailey likely died between 7:50 p.m. and 10:15 p.m. on July 8, a time when there is a 100% certainty that Blaise was in Panaca.

All of the evidence undermining or outright disproving that Blaise had any involvement in Bailey" murder is consistent with the testimony of both a prosecution expert and a defense expert that the severing of Bailey's penis and the slicing across his anus after his death has homosexual overtones. Yet Blaise's prosecution was predicated on the assumption that she killed him while alone – and that was the argument they made to the jury.

The principle of triangulation puts the prosecution's lack of a case against Blaise in perspective. The three critical points are Bailey, Blaise and the crime/crime scene. All three have to intersect for Blaise to be even considered for involvement in Bailey's murder. Yet, at the time of Blaise's retrial – almost 5-1/2 years after Bailey's murder – the prosecution had found *zero* evidence of any association between Bailey and Blaise, even though integral to the prosecution's "theory of the crime" was the allegation that Bailey was dealing methamphetamines to Blaise. The prosecution made that allegation without presenting any evidence that Bailey had ever dealt methamphetamine or any other drug to anyone. Consistent with that absence of evidence is that at the time of Blaise's retrial the prosecution had *zero* evidence that Blaise was at the scene of Bailey's murder, or that she had ever been there at any time. Thus, there was neither any triangulation between Blaise, Bailey and the crime scene to support DiGiacomo's argument that it is "possible" Blaise murdered Bailey, nor to support Kephart's argument that Bailey's murder and the assault on Blaise are too "coincidental" to be considered different events.

Based on the prosecution's case it is neither within the realm of "possibility" that Blaise committed the crime, nor reasonable to reject coincidence as explaining the several details of Bailey's murder and the attempted rape of Blaise that share some inconsequential level of similarity. (That two crimes committed six weeks apart in Las Vegas, a city of half-a-million people, involved an African-American male and a sharp object does not qualify as a coincidence.)

Forensic psychiatrist Dr. Michael Welner told the Las Vegas *Review-Journal* a few days after Blaise's arrest, "This is a very peculiar story. It is the kind of thing that just happens in the movies." [279] A conclusion, indeed the most obvious conclusion as this is written six-and-a-half years after Blaise's arrest, is that the prosecution's case against her is as fictitious as any movie script. The prosecution's theory of her commission of the crime is as far-fetched as any movie's imaginative make-believe plot. Instead of conducting a legitimate investigation to try and apprehend Bailey's murderer(s), in the six-and-a-half years since his murder the prosecution has attempted to close his case by creating a scenario of his death that while fit for a fictional movie, doesn't stand up to any degree of critical real-life scrutiny. The primary beneficiary of the Las Vegas Metropolitan Police Department's failure to investigate Bailey's murder are the persons given a free pass for committing the crime – and who were left on the street to possibly harm other people in Las Vegas or elsewhere. (Based on the cigarette butts found underneath the plastic sheeting covering Bailey's body, we know that at least two people were likely involved in Bailey's murder, and DNA testing establishes that at least one of them is a male.)

The *corpus delicti* rule that predates the founding of the United States, is intended to prevent the prosecution of an innocent person by requiring the State to produce evidence that a person committed a crime independent of anything the person is alleged to have said. [280] The prosecution's case against Blaise is based on interpretations and recollections of extra-judicial statements she is alleged to have made. Blaise's 26-minute recorded statement contains no incriminating information, and none of the recollections of Tienken, Austria, and others, include the many very specific and unusual details of Bailey's murder. (His severed penis was only one of those details.) Yet, apart from those recollections of Blaise's description of a sexual assault in Las Vegas, the prosecution has no evidence – zero – that even suggests she had anything to do with brutally beating, stabbing, and murdering Bailey, and then stabbing and slicing his body and severing his penis. Furthermore, none of those recollections undermines the evidence that Blaise was in Panaca the entire day of July 8, 2001.

An examination of Blaise's case reveals deep flaws in the collection, preservation and testing of evidence, and the investigation, prosecution and adjudication of serious crimes in Clark County, Nevada, and in a larger sense, jurisdictions all across the United States. That is because the same bureaucratic police, prosecution and judicial processes and influences involved in Blaise's case are typical of those that prevail throughout the country. [281] It is sobering to consider, but there is every reason to think Blaise could have been convicted without evidence of her guilt – twice – anywhere else in the country under the same circumstances of an underfunded defense, detectives unconcerned about the truth, prosecutors obsessed with "winning at all costs," law enforcement witnesses willing to fudge the truth or perjure themselves, an overtly prosecution friendly judge who as a former assistant DA intimately worked with the case's lead prosecutor, and jurors who uncritically accept the prosecution's unsubstantiated and illogical assertions that it is possible the defendant is guilty. (It is not yet known if Blaise's conviction after her retrial was partially due to prejudicial juror misconduct, i.e., jurors deciding they were going to vote her guilty prior to the defense presenting its case.)

The cold hard reality is that the standard relied on to support Blaise's prosecution and her convictions after her two trials is not proof of her guilt beyond a reasonable doubt. Rather the standard is it is possible the accusation she murdered Bailey is true. The initial accusation by Johnson was accepted without investigation by Thowsen and LaRochelle, then accepted without critical review by the Clark County District Attorneys Office, then accepted as testimony without evidentiary support by Vega, and then accepted on blind faith by the jurors.

The accusation based proof of guilt upon which Blaise's conviction rests is similar to the spectral evidence that was relied on to convict many thousands of people as witches in England, Scotland, Europe and even in colonial New England. But reliance on an accusation as evidence sufficient for a conviction was repudiated more than 300 years ago by the legal system of the colonies that became the original members of the United States.

Ironically, a person convicted of witchcraft was more likely guilty than Blaise, because they were typically *present* at the alleged crime scene, and they may have *done* something, such as use herbs to concoct an effective home remedy attributed to witchcraft. Blaise was thus convicted on the basis of less evidence of her guilt than was used to convict accused witches in Salem, Massachusetts in 1692.

Yet we know the people convicted of witchcraft were in fact 100% innocent – and there is every reason to conclude after considering the evidence that so is Blaise. When the possibility of guilt is allowed to replace proof beyond a reasonable doubt as the *de facto* standard for a conviction, the result is an unreasonable conviction – such as that of Kirstin Blaise Lobato.

Appeal of retrial conviction

Blaise continues serving her prison sentence as the Nevada Supreme Court considers the direct appeal of her October 2006 convictions. The future will tell if it is decided that one or more legal errors were committed during her retrial that warrants granting her a new trial, or if she will have to pursue habeas corpus proceedings in state and federal court. However the basic facts of her case will remain unchanged regardless of how her appeal based on legal issues turns out, and it will continue on as a case study for how easily the reliance on gossip and innuendo by the police, prosecutors, witnesses, judge and jurors involved in a case can result in an out of control murder prosecution that takes on a life of its own.

Blaise in the late summer of 2006 when she traveled to San Francisco to meet with her *pro bono* attorneys Shari Greenberger and Sara Zalkin prior to her retrial. When will she again be able to do this?

Index

Endnotes

[1] Other people, including Blaise's friend Chris Carrington, have likewise said the detective's pressured them during their interview to alter their recollection to fit what the detective's wanted.

[2] The testimony of Jeremy Davis establishes the assault occurred just before the 2001 Memorial Day weekend. In his statement to the police, Davis said Blaise left her car at his house on Friday, May 25, 2001, the day before the beginning of the Memorial Day weekend. During Blaise's first trial Davis testified she left her car at his house on May 24 or May 25, 2001.

[3] Bailey weighed 133 pounds at the time of his autopsy, and Medical Examiner Lary Simms testified that Bailey lost about two quarts of blood. Blood weighs approximately 8 pounds per gallon, so his lost blood weighed about 4 pounds. Which means he weighed about 137 pounds prior to his murder. *State v. Kirstin Blaise Lobato*, Case Number C177394, Transcript, October 4, 2006, VIII. 78. (The blood on the ground at the time scene was "consistent with about two quarts of blood.")

[4] Statement to Las Vegas Metropolitan Police Department by Richard Shott, Event #010708-2410, 1:23 a.m., July 9, 2001., p. 7. [Hereinafter referred to as "Shott Statement."]

[5] The bank's address is 4240 W. Flamingo Road. The trash enclosure was 10′ wide and 14′ deep with 6′ high walls, and made of concrete blocks. Those are the same dimensions as trash enclosures at the Budget Suites Hotel at 4855 Boulder Highway, where Kirstin Lobato was attacked just before Memorial Day 2001, six weeks before Bailey's murder.

[6] Although there is no reason to doubt the truthfulness of Shott's statement to officers at the crime scene, for reasons unknown, he testified in May 2002 at Kirstin Lobato's trial that he waited for 2-1/2 hours before calling 911. See, *The State of Nevada v. Kirstin Blaise Lobato*, No. C177394, Transcript Vol. 1, 53, Testimony of Richard Shott, May 8, 2002. However, in addition to Shott's statement taken less then three hours after he called 911, in which he said he immediately called 911, LVMPD Homicide Detective James LaRochelle told the coroner's investigator that Shott immediately called 911. The coroner investigator's Summary of Investigation states: "Upon my arrival at approximately 0345 hours, I met with LVMPD Homicide Det. LaRochelle who related the following information to me. A transient known to LVMPD was walking through the parking lot and noticed that the lock was removed from the caged dumpster area. He went into this area and observed the decedent's foot sticking out from underneath the trash that was covering him. He walked to a telephone and called 911." Summary of Investigation, Shelley Pierce-Stauffer, Clark County Coroner, *Report of Investigation*, No. 01-04231, 3:50 a.m., July 9, 2001. Homicide Detectives LaRochelle and Thomas Thowsen also wrote that after discovery of the body Shott immediately called 911. See, Las Vegas Metropolitan Police Department, *Continuation Report*, Event #010708-2410, August 22, 2001.

[7] Office James Testa testified he received the emergency call at about 10:45 p.m., and it took him three to four minutes to arrive at the scene. *State v. Kirstin Blaise Lobato*, Case Number C177394, Transcript, September 14, 2006, IV. 109-110.

[8] *State v. Kirstin Blaise Lobato*, Case Number C177394, Transcript, September 14, 2006, IV. 116. Direct examination.

[9] Bailey was arrested by the LVMPD at least one time, on October 18, 1999. (See the booking photo on page 8.) *Justice:Denied* submitted a Public Records request to the LVMPD for Bailey's arrest record for that incident, but the police department refused to provide the record. At the time this is written in February 2008 a request *Justice:Denied* submitted to the FBI for Bailey's file is pending.

[10] The Clark County DAs office has never contended that the bloody shoeprints were made by either Shott, or anyone else after the first officers arrived at 10:50 p.m.

[11] Autopsy Report: Pathologic Examination On The Body Of Duran Bailey, Clark County Coroner, July 9, 2001 (Las Vegas, NV).

[12] *Id.*

[13] Simms expressed that opinion during Kirstin "Blaise" Lobato's Preliminary Hearing on August 7, 2001, based on the fact that when he performed the autopsy, "The body wasn't manifesting any significant degree of decomposition, so I would say he had died a lot closer to the time he was discovered than not." See, *State v. Lobato*, Case No. C177394, Reporter's Transcript of Preliminary Hearing, August 7, 2001, 32-33.

Although the information upon which Simms based his initial estimate remained unchanged, during the next five years Simms thrice revised his estimate of Bailey's time of death. He did so in April 2002 during Blaise's first trial, when he changed Bailey's estimated time of death to between 8 and 18 hours from the time of the first officer's arrival on the scene. Officer Testa arrived at about 10:50 a.m., so his death would have been between 2:50 p.m. and 4:50 a.m. on July 8. Then in September 2006 during Blaise's retrial, he again revised his time of death estimate to "possibly" being between 8 and 24 hours from the time the coroner's investigator examined Bailey at the crime scene. That revision means Bailey could have died from 7:50 p.m. to 3:50 a.m. on July 8. However, Simms qualified his September 2006 estimate by testifying that "to a reasonable medical certainty" Bailey's time of death was likely 12-18 hours from the time of the crime scene examination – which would be from 3:50 p.m. to 9:50 a.m. on the 8th.

[14] "If you're looking at for instance to discern if somebody died at 12:00 o'clock or 1:00 o'clock." See, *State v. Lobato*, Case No. C177394, Reporter's Transcript of Preliminary Hearing, August 7, 2001, 24.

[15] *State v. Lobato*, Case No. C177394, Reporter's Transcript of Preliminary Hearing, August 7, 2001, 24, 32-33.

[16] Michael M. Baden and Judith Adler Hennessee, M.D., *Unnatural Death – Confessions of a Medical Examiner*, Random House, 1989, pg. 96.

[17] The Grand View Apartments address is 4255 W Viking Rd Las Vegas, NV 89103-5906. The southern boundary of the Grand View Apartments is about 200 feet north of the Nevada State Bank.

[18] *The State of Nevada v. Kirstin Blaise Lobato*, No. C177394, Transcript Vol. 5, 13, Testimony of Diann Parker, May 14, 2002.

[19] *Id.* at 45.

[20] *Id.* at 46.

[21] *Id.* at 23.

[22] *Id.* at 12-28.

[23] Crime in the United States 2001, Uniform Crime Reports, Federal Bureau of Investigation, U.S. Department of Justice, Washington D.C., Table 2.12.

[24] Bailey lived at the Grand View Apartments with his mother until her death.

[25] The irony of detective Thowsen and LaRochelle's failure to pursue investigating Parker and her male acquaintances as suspects is that if they had been charged with Bailey's first-degree murder, there is reason to believe they could have been convicted on the basis of the substantial circumstantial evidence suggesting they were involved in Bailey's death, and that they had the motive, means and opportunity to do so. Particularly considering Kirstin "Blaise" Lobato was convicted twice – first in May 2002 and again in October 2006 – while lacking any of those factors.

[26] During Blaise's retrial, Maria Thomas testified:

Q. Okay. Now, you had another task in this case as well. Do you remember traveling to Panaca, Nevada, on the 20th of July, 2001?

A. Yes,

Q. Okay. And what was the reason for you going to Panaca, Nevada?

A. The homicide detectives assigned to the case had asked me to go with them to take photographs of Ms, Lobato, and also to follow the vehicle back to the crime lab. There was a particular vehicle that the detectives wanted followed and processed. So my job in this particular case was to follow the vehicle back to the lab and turn it over to the crime scene investigator that would have processed that vehicle. (XI-57)

Q. Did you travel with the homicide detectives to Panaca or did you drive in your own car?

A. I drove in my own car.

Q. Okay. Were you requested to come up to Panaca,

Nevada, after the detectives were there or did you follow them?

A. I followed them. (XI-58)

State v. Kirstin Blaise Lobato, Case Number C177394, Transcript, September 25, 2006, XI. 57-58. (Direct examination by Kephart.)

[27] Johnson falsely stated twice that Blaise had been on probation with her as Blaise's supervisor. First on page 3 ("Uh, she told me about a girl that I used to have on probation, a Blaise Lobato ..."), and second on page 7 ("And I know when she was on probation with me a few years ago ..."). Statement to Las Vegas Metropolitan Police Department by Laura Linn Johnson, Event #010708-2410, July 20, 2001, pp. 2-3. [Hereinafter referred to as "Johnson's Statement."]

[28] The Lincoln County District Attorney provided that information in a letter to The Justice Institute/*Justice:Denied* dated January 4, 2007. The letter was in response to a Public Disclosure Act request.

[29] Among the inconsistencies between what Johnson told the detectives and the subsequent statements by Blaise and Dixie that would have been a red flag about Johnson's veracity if the detectives had conducted an investigation before deciding on Blaise's guilt, is that Johnson said Dixie said the attack on Blaise occurred as she "was coming out of a strip club ... and a man attacked her and he had his, uh, penis hanging out of his pants." Johnson's Statement at 3. That description of the attack neither bears any resemblance to the location or type of assault that Blaise described in her statement of July 20, 2001, or that Dixie described in her statement of July 26, 2001, nor does it resemble the location of Bailey's murder or the type of attack that resulted in his death.

[30] The Budget Suites Hotel is at 4855 Boulder Highway. Dixie Tienken testified that based on her conversation with Blaise she believed the man was "over 6 foot tall, over 200 pounds. ... And she also said he was old."
State v. Kirstin Blaise Lobato, Case Number C177394, Transcript, September 15, 2006, V. 68.

[31] This relating of events is a composite of Blaise's statement to Detectives Thowsen and LaRochelle on July 20, 2001, and conversations she had with other people. See, Statement to Las Vegas Metropolitan Police Department by Kirsten Blaise Lobato, Event #010708-2410, July 20, 2001. [Hereinafter referred to as "Blaise's Statement."] The testimony of Jeremy Davis establishes the assault occurred on May 23, 24 or 25, just before the 2001 Memorial Day weekend. In his statement to the police, Davis said Blaise left her car at his house on Friday, May 25, 2001, the day before the beginning of the Memorial Day weekend. During Blaise's first trial Davis testified she left her car at his house on May 24 or May 25, 2001.

[32] The police statement and testimony of Jeremy Davis establishes the assault occurred on May 23, 24 or 25, just before the 2001 Memorial Day weekend.

[33] "Rights of Persons Arrested," signed by Kirstin "Blaise" Lobato, 7-20-01, 5:55 p.m., witnessed by T. Thowsen 1407, Las Vegas Metropolitan Police Department.

[34] Crime in the United States 2001, Uniform Crime Reports, Federal Bureau of Investigation, U.S. Department of Justice, Washington D.C., Table 6, Index of Crime by Metropolitan Statistical Area, 2001.

[35] *Id.*, Table 2.13, Murder Circumstances (There were 13,752 murders and 1,796 were committed by a knife or other cutting object.), p. 26.

[36] *Id.*, Table 2.24, Aggravated Assault, Types of Weapons Used p. 38.

[37] In July 2001 blacks comprised 10.4% of Las Vegas population of 503,000, and Las Vegas is a large city of 84 square miles.

[38] The *Miranda* waiver Blaise signed at 5:55 p.m. soon after the detectives arrived at the home of her parents, and which she signed twelve minutes before Thowsen turned his tape recorder on, specifically states that the written waiver is for a person under arrest.

[39] The arrest report written by LaRochelle doesn't contain any corroborative information. See, Arrest Report, ID/Event No. 1691351, Lobato, Kirstin Blaise, July 20, 2001, LVMPD.

[40] *The State of Nevada v. Kirstin Blaise Lobato*, No. 01F12209X, Dept. 2, Criminal Complaint, July 23, 2001.

[41] *The State of Nevada v. Kirstin Blaise Lobato*, No. 01F12209X, Dept. 2, Amended Criminal Complaint, July 26, 2001.

[42] Statement to Las Vegas Metropolitan Police Department by Dixie Tienken, Event #010708-2410, July 26, 2001. (Hereinafter referred to as, "Tienken's Statement.")

[43] *Id.* at 9-10. ("She said she saw him stumbling and getting up, and she said stumbling and getting up." *Id.* at 10)

[44] *Id.* at 4.

[45] "I don't know that it was really completely separate because Blaze has a way or coloring her stories." *Id.* at 25.

[46] *Id.* at 5 and 11.

[47] *Id.* at 21.

[48] *Id.* at 24.

[49] These statements were made during a telephone interview of Dixie Tienken by Hans Sherrer on January 6, 2007.

[50] Peter O'Connell, "Murder Charge: Cut Result of Attack, Teen Says," Las Vegas *Review-Journal*, July 25, 2001.

[51] Larry Lobato testimony on October 3, 2006, at retrial of Kirstin Blaise Lobato.

[52] Arrest Report, Event ID No. 1691351, Kirstin Blaise Lobato, July 22, 2001. Interestingly, the arrest report lists Bailey's time of death as 2236, or 10:36 p.m. on July 8. That was the time the 911 call was received from Richard Shott reporting that he had found a body.

[53] William J Bodziak, Footwear Examination Report, Forensic Consultant Services, March 27, 2002.

[54] Blaise's Statement, *supra*.

[55] It would have been inaccurate if Blaise had said it occurred "over two months ago." So her statement can be inferred to mean "over a month ago" but less than two months ago, which is accurate.

[56] Simms testified on cross-examination that Bailey lost about two quarts of blood, and acknowledged that the blood on the ground at the time scene was "consistent with about two quarts of blood." *State v. Kirstin Blaise Lobato*, Case Number C177394, Transcript, October 4, 2006, VIII. 78. Blood weighs approximately 8-1/2 pounds per gallon.

[57] Dixie Tienken testified that based on her conversation with Blaise she believed the man was "over 6 foot tall, over 200 pounds. ... And she also said he was old." *State v. Kirstin Blaise Lobato*, Case Number C177394, Transcript, September 15, 2006, V. 68.

[58] Blaise's Statement, *supra*, at 4.

[59] *Id.*, at 11.

[60] William J Bodziak, "Footwear Examination Report," Forensic Consultant Services, March 27, 2002.

[61] *Id.*

[62] *Id.*

[63] Blaise's Statement, *supra*, at 12.

[64] *Id.*

[65] *Id.* at 3.

[66] *Id.* at 24.

[67] The lab test was conducted on July 7 by a laboratory in Las Vegas.

[68] Blaise's Statement, *supra*, at 4. See also,

Q. (by Thowsen) And what area, what type of area were you in? Were you in an open parking lot where people could see you or were you in ...

A. Yeah it was a parking lot but it was dark and it was late. *Id.* at 7

[69] *Id.* at 4. See also,

Q. (by Thowsen) And what area, what type of area were you in? Were you in an open parking lot where people could see you or were you in ...

A. Yeah it was a parking lot but it was dark and it was late. *Id.* at 7

[70] A.B. 287, *Assembly History, Sixty-second session*, State of Nevada, p. 107. (Special thanks to Michelle Ravell for researching and obtaining the legislative history of A.B. 287.

The proposed bill, which was enacted without any changes read:

1. A person who commits a sexual penetration on the dead body of a human being is guilty of a category A felony and shall be punished by imprisonment in the state prison for life with the possibility of parole, with eligibility for parole beginning when a minimum of 5 years has been served, and shall be further punished by a fine of not more than $20,000.

2. For the purposes of this section, "sexual penetration" means cunnilingus, fellatio or any intrusion, however slight, of any part of a person's body or any object manipulated or inserted by a person into the genital or anal openings of the body of another, including, without limitation, sexual intercourse in what would be its ordinary meaning if practiced upon the living.

[71] A.B. 287, Assembly Judiciary Committee, Minutes of the Nevada State Legislature, March 16, 1983, 988. (Emphasis added to original.)

[72] Rape is defined as, "Nonconsensual sexual penetration of an individual, obtained by force or threat, or in cases in which the victim is not capable of consent." *Dorland's Illustrated Medical Dictionary, 31st Edition*, (Philadelphia: Saunders/Elsevier (2004)), 1617.

[73] *Id.* at 788.

[74] *Id.* at 789.

[75] NRS 201.450(2). The statute states in part: "sexual penetration" means cunnilingus, fellatio or any intrusion, however slight, of any part of a person's body or any object manipulated or inserted by a person into the genital or anal openings of the body of another, including, without limitation, sexual intercourse in what would be its ordinary meaning if practiced upon the living."

[76] A.B. 287, Senate Judiciary Hearing, Minutes of the Nevada State Legislature, April 5, 1983, 788.

[77] NRS 201.450(2)

[78] The only difference between the definition of "sexual penetration" of a living "person" (in NRS 200.364) and of a corpse in the necrophilia law, is that the latter includes the two words "without limitation," preceding "sexual intercourse in its ordinary meaning if practiced upon the living."

The legislative history of the necrophilia law doesn't provide a clue as to what the two additional words mean, however, since they are immediately followed by "sexual intercourse," it is reasonable to assume they directly relate to sex related act, which assumption is consistent with the Assembly and Senate committee testimony concerning the purpose and intent of the necrophilia law to criminalize the same sex acts committed with a corpse as with a living person.

[79] necrophilia, n., Draft Revision Sept. 2003, *Oxford English Dictionary Online*, http://dictionary.oed.com (last visited January 23, 2008). The *Oxford English Dictionary* is the world's most authoritative English dictionary.

[80] During Blaise's Preliminary Hearing on August 7, 2001, Simms testified in regards to Bailey's autopsy. The following exchanges occurred on direct examination by Assistant D.A. Eric Jorgensen:

"Q. Now, what were the – what did you find on external examination?

A. [by Simms] Well, *there was dozens of injuries*. Do you want me to go into each individually or sum them up?

Q. Would you sum them up?

A. There was a number of blunt force injuries all over the head and face. And there was a number of sharp force injuries including slash wounds and stab wounds that involved the neck, face; there were defensive wounds on the hands; there was a stab wound in the abdomen; and there was some sexual mutilation, the penis was amputated; *there was a large slash wound in the rectal area*." See, *State v. Lobato*, Case No. C177394, Reporter's Transcript of Preliminary Hearing, August 7, 2001, 19.

Simms testified about the "slash wound" to Bailey's rectal area during an additional five exchanges with the assistant district attorney.

[81] *Doyle v. State,* 112 Nev. 879, 900 n.8, 921 P.2d 901, 914 n.8 (1996). (Referring to the plain meaning of NRS 201.450.)

[82] After Blaise's May 2002 conviction of first-degree murder and necrophilia, her lawyers raised the ground of error in her appeal, and argued in their brief to the Nevada Supreme Court, that the necrophilia law was unconstitutionally applied and is void for vagueness. They did not, however, include any research about the legislative history or intent of the legislature in enacting the necrophilia law, consequently the Court's rejection of the claim was not based on the substantive merits that the law has no applicability to the facts of Bailey's murder. See, *Lobato v. State*, 96 P.3d 765 (Nev. 09/03/2004), ¶42.

[83] When Thowsen interviewed Twining he was told by Twining about the phone records. Twining attempted to give him the records, but Thowsen wasn't interested in the records that corroborated Blaise's presence in Panaca on July 2 to July 9.

[84] *The State of Nevada v. Kirstin Blaise Lobato*, No. C177394, Transcript Vol. 3, 169, Testimony of Korinda Martin, May 10, 2002.

[85] Crime in the United States 2001, Uniform Crime Reports, Federal Bureau of Investigation, U.S. Department of Justice, Washington D.C., Table 6, Index of Crime (There were 447 *reported* rapes in Las Vegas in 2001.).

[86] *Id.* (There were 133 identifiable murders in Las Vegas in 2001).

[87] *Id.*, Table 2.9, Murder, Types of Weapons Used. (A sharp object (knife, scissors, etc.) was involved in 13% of all murders, and 24% of murders were committed with fists or an unknown weapon.)

[88] The address of the Budget Suites is 4855 Boulder Highway, Las Vegas. The Las Vegas Metropolitan Police Department Website, Crime View Community at, http://www.lvmpd.com/crimeviewcommunity/. The reported crimes were, Assault/Battery, Burglary, Robbery, and Stolen Motor Vehicle. For comparison's sake, in the 60 days preceding November 4, 2004, there were 102 of the same crimes reported and 44 assaults.

[89] The address of the Nevada State Bank is 4240 W. Flamingo Road, Las Vegas. Thirty seven of the reported crimes were assaults. *Id.* . For comparison's sake, in the 60 days preceding November 4, 2004, there were 157 of the same crimes reported, that included 58 assaults.

[90] Glenn Puit, "'Sensitive' Defendant Denies Mutilation Slaying Charge," Las Vegas *Review-Journal*, May 16, 2002.

[91] "Reporting to the police," 2001 National Crime Victimization Survey, Bureau of Justice Statistics (U. S. Department of Justice), p. 10. At, http://www.ojp.gov/bjs/pub/pdf/cv01.pdf

[92] Kephart didn't just argue this in court, but explained it to journalists during the jurors deliberations, and then after Blaise was sentenced on August 28, 2002. See, Glenn Puit, "Homeless man's killer sentenced," Las Vegas *Review-Journal*, August 28, 2002; and, Glenn Puit, "Jurors Deliberate Severed Penis Slaying," Las Vegas *Review-Journal*, May 17, 2002.

[93] Johnson's Statement, *supra*, at 11.

[94] The July 7, 2001 tests of the July 5 blood sample were conducted by Associated Pathologists Laboratories, 4230 Burnham Ave., Las Vegas. The test detected marijuana in her system, but no other drug.

[95] *State v. Kirstin Blaise Lobato*, Case Number C177394, Transcript, May 10, 2002, III. 169, 172, 175. See also, Informant: Lobato Boasted; Inmate Kept log of her conversations with murder suspect, Las Vegas *Review-Journal*, May 11, 2002, ("She was boasting about it.").

[96] Peter O'Connell, "Murder Charge: Cut Result of Attack, Teen Says," Las Vegas *Review-Journal*, July 25, 2001.

[97] *Lobato v. State*, 96 P.3d 765 (Nev. 09/03/2004)

[98] Glenn Puit, "Convicted Killer Turned Down Plea Deal," Las Vegas *Review-Journal*, May 29, 2002.

[99] *Lobato v. State*, 96 P.3d 765 (Nev. 09/03/2004)

[100] *Id.*

[101] *Id.*

[102] Glenn Puit, "Convicted Killer Turned Down Plea Deal," Las Vegas *Review-Journal*, May 29, 2002.

[103] Autopsy Report, *supra*.

[104] *The State of Nevada v. Kirstin Blaise Lobato*, No. C177394, Transcript Vol. 2, 38, Testimony of Lary Simms, May 9, 2002.

[105] *Id.* at 39.

[106] *The State of Nevada v. Kirstin Blaise Lobato*, No. C177394, Transcript Vol. 4, 124, Testimony of Thomas Wahl, May 13, 2002.

[107] See the AFDAA website at, http://www.afdaa.org/index.html (last visited November 4, 2004).

[108] Crime Scene Reconstruction and Forensic Science Interpretation in *State v. Kirstin Lobato*, Case No. C177394. Forensic Science Resources, Case No. FSR2-02, May 31, 2002, p. 3. (Bold in original.) This report was completed after Blaise's trial.

[109] See e.g., "Expert's Testimony Limited," Las Vegas *Review-Journal*, May 17, 2002.

[110] Crime Scene Reconstruction and Forensic Science Interpretation in *State v. Kirstin Lobato*, Case No. C177394. Forensic Science Resources, Case No. FSR2-02, May 31, 2002, p. 3.

[111] *Id.* at 3. (Bold in original.)

[112] *Id.* at 3. (Bold in original.)

[113] *Id.* at 3.

[114] *Id.* at 3.

[115] *Id.* at 3.

[116] *Id.* at 3.

[117] *Id.* at 1-2, 4.

[118] *Id.* at 3-4. (emphasis added to original.) Schiro's reconstruction of Bailey's murder that portrays it as a premeditated event is wholly incompatible with the prosecution's theory of the crime. The prosecution's scenario depends on their supposition that Blaise went to see Bailey to buy methamphetamines, and that his murder was a consequence of her becoming hysterically violent after taking that meth.

[119] In his report, Schiro summarized his finding about the alleged blood in her car, "Based on the results of the phenolphthalein, luminol, human hemoglobin, and human DNA quantification analyses, the substance detected in Ms. Lobato's vehicle is not human blood." Crime Scene Reconstruction and Forensic Science Interpretation in *State v. Kirstin Lobato*, Case No. C177394. Forensic Science Resources, Case No. FSR2-02, May 31, 2002, p. 4.

[120] "Expert's Testimony Limited," Las Vegas *Review-Journal*, May 17, 2002. (emphasis added).

[121] Crime Scene Reconstruction and Forensic Science Interpretation in *State v. Kirstin Lobato*, Case No. C177394. Forensic Science Resources, Case No. FSR2-02, May 31, 2002, p. 5.

[122] *State v. Kirstin Blaise Lobato*, Case Number C177394, Transcript, May 17, 2002, VIII – 109.

[123] *Id.* at 130.

[124] The jury provided proof positive at 1:23 a.m. that the prosecution's strategy of demonizing Blaise and her family had worked magnificently. The jury foreman, Clarence Templeton, sent a note to Judge Vega that stated: "We are concerned about repercussions from the Lobato family and our future security." About forty-five minutes later the jury informed the bailiff that they had reached a verdict.

[125] Glenn Puit, "Convicted Killer Turned Down Plea Deal," Las Vegas *Journal-Review*, May 29, 2002.

[126] As of December 1, 2007 the website is still online at, http://www.angelfire.com/stars4/justiceforkirstin

[127] The article is at, http://www.justicedenied.org/issue/issue_26/kl/kirstin_lobato_jd_issue26.html (last visited December 1, 2007). A follow-up article, *Possibility Of Guilt Replaces Proof Beyond A Reasonable Doubt*, focused on her retrial in Sept. and October 2006. Published in the Fall 2006 issue (Issue 34), that article is at, http://justicedenied.org/issue/issue_34/lobato_jd34.htm (last visited December 1, 2007).

[128] *Lobato v. State*, 96 P.3d 765 (Nev. 09/03/2004)

[129] *Id.*

[130] *Id.*

[131] *Id.*

[132] Judge Vega was a "Clark County Deputy District Attorney from 1984 through 1989, prosecuting felony cases, and was instrumental in implementing the office's first Sexual Assault and Child Abuse team." At the age of 33, Vega was "appointed to the Clark County Municipal Court in 1989 and was retained and re-elected by the voters until her resignation in 1999 to accept the District Court appointment." See, Eighth Judicial District Court Biographies, http://www.co.clark.nv.us/District_Court/bios.htm (last visited December 30, 2006.)

[133] Defendant Lobato's Notice Of Motion And Motion In Limine To Exclude Testimony Of Laura Johnson, *State v. Lobato*, No C177394, District Court, Clark County, NV, p. 10.

[134] *Id.* at 12.

[135] Those two spots where on the drivers side door and on the seat cover.

[136] Forensic Examination Report, Kirstin "Blaise" Lobato Case, By Brent Turvey, October 17, 2005, p. 5, see also, 3-4. Another strong argument undermining the alleged use of cleaning agents (such as bleach) is their use would have left some trace of discoloration on the surface cleaned – but there was none.

[137] Defendant Lobato's Notice Of Motion And Motion In Limine To Exclude Inflammatory and Cumulative Photographs, *State v. Lobato*, Case No. C177394, Dept II, District Court, Clark County, Nevada, p. 4.

[138] The license plate read, 4NIK8ER. Blaise's dad Larry Lobato testified during her retrial that he suggested the custom plate to Blaise when he was joking around with her. *State v. Kirstin Blaise Lobato*, Case Number C177394, Transcript, October 4, 2006, XVIII. 25-26. (cross-examination)

[139] Blaise's car was so mechanically unreliable that it broke down in May 2001 on her way to Las Vegas after she stayed in Panaca for two weeks around Mother's Day. Dixie Tienken mentioned in her statement of July 26, 2001 that Blaise's car had "broken down" while she was in Las Vegas.

[140] Recorder's Transcript Of Hearing Of All Pending Motions, *State v. Lobato*, Case No. C177394, Dept II, District Court, Clark County, Nevada, May 19, 2006., p. 39.

[141] The first felony (murder) conviction in the United States attributable to fingerprint identification was in Illinois in 1910. Simon A. Cole, *Suspect Identities: A History of Fingerprinting and Criminal Identification* 177 (Harvard University Press 2001).

[142] *CSI: Crime Scene Investigations* official website is, http://www.cbs.com/primetime/csi/

[143] Kirstin Lobato's Motion To Dismiss Because The State Cannot Establish The Corpus Delicti Of The Crime With Evidence Independent Of Defendant's Extrajudicial Admissions, *State v. Lobato*, Case No. C177394, Dept II, District Court, Clark County, Nevada.

[144] *Id.* at 6.

[145] The 'corpus delicti rule' is centuries old, dating from the English common law. Washington State's rule was used in the case of convicted killer and kidnapper Joseph Duncan III. Duncan allegedly confessed to murdering two young girls in Seattle, Washington in 1996, but there is no other evidence he committed the crimes. Consequently, in January 2007, a King County Sheriff spokesperson told the *Seattle Times*, that charges cannot be filed against Duncan based solely on the confession information, "Such a reported confession is not enough to win a criminal case. Anyone can confess to a murder, but you can't prosecute someone based just on that." Duncan did seem to have knowledge of the crime, "but he could have got that from a cellmate." "No evidence to blame Duncan for girls' deaths, sheriff says," by Natalie Singer (staff), *Seattle Times*, January 26, 2007, B5. Complementing Nevada and Washington's rule, is it was nationally reported in August 2007 that Colorado refused to prosecute John Mark Karr for any involvement in JonBenet Ramsey's

murder because there is no evidence absent his confession. In addition, the available crime scene evidence excludes John Mark Karr. See e.g., Karr cleared in JonBenet Ramsey case, *MSNBC website*, August 28, 2006. The prosecutors wrote in their motion to dismiss the charges, "because no evidence has developed, other than his own repeated admissions, to place Mr. Karr at the scene of the crime and, in particular, because his DNA does not match that found in the victim's blood in her underwear, the People would not be able to establish that Mr. Karr committed this crime despite his repeated insistence that he did." People's Motion To Quash Arrest Warrant, *People v John Mark Karr*, District Court of Boulder County, Colorado, August 28, 2006.

[146] Defendant Lobato's Notice Of Motion And Motion In Limine To Exclude Witness Korinda Martin's Testimony ..., *State v. Kirstin Lobato*, Case No. C177394 ("...the presentation of said testimony is tantamount to suborning perjury.")

[147] *State v. Kirstin Blaise Lobato*, Case Number C177394, Transcript, September 20, 2006, VIII. 6-7. Cross-examination.

[148] *State v. Kirstin Blaise Lobato*, Case Number C177394, Transcript, September 19, 2006, VII. 137.

[149] *State v. Kirstin Blaise Lobato*, Case Number C177394, Transcript, September 20, 2006, VIII. 8. Cross-examination.

[150] Simms testimony about Bailey's time of death is at, *State v. Kirstin Blaise Lobato*, Case Number C177394, Transcript, September 19, 2006, VII. 146:

Q. Okay. Could you give us a -- can you calculate or give us a time of when you believe that Duran Bailey was killed?

A. Well, just based on the rigor mortis that was present

at the scene and the level of decomposition that I saw, I thought a good interval where I would have a good chance of being right would be anywhere from 8 to 24 hours prior to when they did the examination on him.

Q. When you say they?

A. The coroner investigator.

Q. Okay. So that would be 3:50, the time –

A. Somewhere in that area –

Simms also, to Kephart's chagrin, explained that the heat of the Las Vegas summer and the retention of heat by the covering of Bailey's body would have accelerated the rigor mortis process, which would mean that he actually died closer to the time his body was examined than reflected in his estimate. See, *Id.* at 147-149.

[151] *State v. Kirstin Blaise Lobato*, Case Number C177394, Transcript, September 20, 2006, VIII. 24:

Q. Okay, So our 12 to 18 before 3:50 is pretty fair to a reasonable medical certainty?

A. I believe it is, yes,

Q. Okay. And 12 hours prior to 3:50 a.m. would be 3:50 p.m.?

A. P.m., right.

Q. Okay. Which would be 3:50 in the afternoon?

A. Correct.

The most remote estimated time of death of 3:50 a.m. was Simms' third time under oath he had given a different estimate of Bailey's earliest possible time of death. At the August 2001 preliminary hearing his estimate of Bailey's most remote time of death meant he did not die prior to 10:50 a.m., during Blaise's May 2002 trial his testimony established Bailey's most remote time of death would have been 4:50 a.m., and during Blaise's retrial he estimated Bailey's most remote time of death was 3:50 a.m. Simms' "gaming" of Bailey's most remote time of death after his preliminary hearing testimony was critical for Blaise's prosecution, because in her statement she said she was attacked during very early morning hours (shortly after midnight). Simms' expanding of Bailey's possible time of death to pre-dawn on July 8, although not as early as Blaise said she was attacked, nevertheless enabled prosecutors DiGiacomo and Kephart to argue that the nighttime assault on Blaise and Bailey's death were the same event.

[152] An unexplained inconsistency in Simms' testimony, along with altering Bailey's time of death, is he testified at Blaise's retrial that the "blunt force trauma" head wounds occurred some time prior to him dying from the stabbing wounds, while in his autopsy report Simms' concluded the trauma wounds caused his death.

[153] Simms, however, hedged his testimony by saying at the urging of the prosecution that it was "possible" Bailey's head and facial injuries could have been caused by a bat swung with very little force.

[154] Simms again hedged his testimony by agreeing with the prosecution's assertion that it was "possible" an object with a shorter blade inflicted Bailey's cutting and stabbing injuries.

[155] *State v. Kirstin Blaise Lobato*, Case Number C177394, Transcript, September 15, 2006, V. 173.

[156] *Id.* at 174.

[157] *Id.* at 174-175.

[158] It is unknown when this conversation took place. During a January 6, 2007, telephone interview with Hans Sherrer, Dixie Tienken said that after the morning conversation with Blaise, the first Wednesday she was in Pioche to teach her once a week GED class at the county jail was July 11, 2001. She stopped by juvenile probation officer Laura Johnson's office on the 11th to talk about her conversation with Blaise. Dixie said that Johnson wasn't in her office so she left a note. The following Wednesday, July 18, 2001, when

she was back in Pioche to teach her weekly GED class, Dixie stopped in and talked with Johnson. Dixie says she cannot remember the day she talked with Blaise, although she does remember it was in the morning. It is known that Blaise was in Las Vegas from the very early morning hours of July 9 to the afternoon of July 13, so Blaise only could have talked to her on one of the mornings from July 3 to July 8 when she was in Panaca. (There would have been no GED class at the county jail on Wednesday, July 4.)

[159] *State v. Kirstin Blaise Lobato*, Case Number C177394, Transcript, September 15, 2006, V. 52.

[160] *State v. Kirstin Blaise Lobato*, Case Number C177394, Transcript, September 27, 2006, XIII. 158.

[161] Reducing a Guilty Suspect's Resistance to Confessing: Applying Criminological Theory to Interrogation Theme Development, By Brian Parsi Boetig, M.S., *FBI Law Enforcement Bulletin*, August 2005 Volume 74 Number 8, United States Department of Justice Federal Bureau of Investigation Washington, DC 20535-0001. (Emphasis added to original.) See, http://www.fbi.gov/publications/leb/2005/august2005/august05leb.htm (last visited January 8, 2007)

[162] Lincoln County, Nevada, Wikipedia.com (last visited January 8, 2007). Lincoln County, Nevada is larger than seven states, and has a population density of less than 1/2 person per sq. mi.

[163] Jeremy Davis lived on the Las Vegas' eastside at 4827 Meredith Ave., Las Vegas, NV 89121. This was about 1 mile from the Budget Suites Hotel. From the time of Blaise's arrest to the time of Dixie's statement, the two did not communicate with each other. Dixie didn't even know why Blaise had been arrested until she read the July 25 article in the Las Vegas *Review Journal*.

[164] The parking of Blaise's car is further corroborated by a tow receipt for her car dated June 6, 2001, that was paid by her friend Steve Pyszkowski.

[165] Although Blaise's non-incriminatory statement played no role in her arrest, Thowsen's primary value in her prosecution was successfully obtaining her statement before she could invoke her right to the assistance of counsel, because it enabled the prosecution to argue, however erroneously, that her statement constituted a confession, even though it had no identifiable details relating to Bailey's murder.

[166] Thowsen testimony was somewhat disingenuous because Blaise said in her statement that her attacker was alive when she left, so he likely experienced a wound that may or may not have required professional treatment. Thowsen didn't testify that he made any attempt to investigate the treatment of all knife wounds to a black man in late May 2001, but Las Vegas medical facilities and doctors may still have those records available for examination.

[167] *CSI: Crime Scene Investigations* official website is, http://www.cbs.com/primetime/csi/

[168] *Justice:Denied* has been told, but not from an official source on the record, that budgetary constraints were a consideration in Schiro not being retained for Blaise's retrial. The defense's deficient funding resulted in Dr. Laufer providing his expertise *pro bono*.

[169] A device Laufer invented and co-developed, a catheter-based procedure for the treatment for asthma, was awarded the 2006 Popular Science Best of What's New Award in the Personal Health category. See, Asthmatx, Inc.'s Alair(R) System Named "Best Of 2006" By Popular Science, (BUSINESS WIRE), November 8, 2006.

[170] Michael D. Laufer, MD, *Report Re: Lobato*, September 24, 2006, Interpretation of findings, No. 8., p. 3.

[171] *Id.*, Conclusions, No. 5., p. 4.

[172] *Id.*, Interpretation of findings, No. 5., p. 3.

[173] This conclusion undermines the prosecution's key speculation that Bailey's anus was stabbed after his death, which is the basis of the charge of, "sexual penetration of a dead body."

[174] Brent E. Turvey MS, *Forensic Examination Report*, October 17, 2005, p. 2

[175] *Id.* at 3.

[176] *State v. Kirstin Blaise Lobato*, Case Number C177394, Transcript, October 2, 2006, XVI. 117.

[177] *Id.* at 119.

[178] The following exchange took place during DiGiacomo's cross-examination of Turvey:

Q By Ms. DiGiacomo

A By Brent Turvey

...

Q. Okay. What type of cleaning agent would it take to clean blood out of a car so that it doesn't react with luminal or phenolphthalein?

...

[XVII-28]

...

A. ... There needs to be multiple repeated attempts at cleaning with heavy cleaners, such as a combination of bleach and ethanol – excuse me – and other industrial level cleaners, and it has to be repeated to multiple. Now on a hard surface or nonporous surface, that may do the job. On a porous surface, it's unlikely that even that level of cleaning will get it out enough to the point where luminol would fail to detect it. Again, we're talking one parts per million. And I –

Q. So in this case it is not even an option that the car might've been cleaned and there might've been some blood there that reacted with the luminol or the phenolphthalein but couldn't be confirmed?

Ms. Zalkin: Your Honor, I'm gonna object, asked and answered.

The Court: Overruled. You may answer

The Witness: That is my opinion, And again, the level of cleaning that's required is not small or minor.

By Ms. DiGiacomo:

Q. Now with regard to the bat found in the car, and you said that there's no blood on it whatsoever, based on the

[XVII-29]

fact that they could not do any sort of even presumptive positive test regarding the phenolphthalein?

A. That's correct.

Q. Okay.

A. Not only was there no blood there, there likely was no blood there at any time.

Q. Okay. So the only thing you can say about that bat is that at no time did it have any blood on it, correct?

A. That's correct.

[XVII-30]

State v. Kirstin Blaise Lobato, Case Number C177394, Transcript, October 3, 2006, XVII. 28-30.

[179] It is likely that Blaise's conversation with Dixie was also prior to Bailey's death. See endnote 157.

[180] Pyszkowski's testimony about this is at, *State v. Kirstin Blaise Lobato*, Case Number C177394, Transcript, September 18, 2006, VI. 8-9.

[181] Pyszkowski's testimony on cross-examination about Blaise helping him is at, *Id.* at 24-26.

[182] *State v. Kirstin Blaise Lobato*, Case Number C177394, Transcript, September 18, 2006, VI. 26. See also, VI. 11. See also, Q. Are there portions missing from that statement that you told the police?

A. Yes. I don't believe everything we talked about is in here. *Id.* at 29.

[183] *Id.* at 27.

[184] *Id.* at 28.

[185] *State v. Kirstin Blaise Lobato*, Case Number C177394, Transcript, May 8, 2002, V. I-158-161.

[186] *State v. Kirstin Blaise Lobato*, Case Number C177394, Transcript, May 10, 2002, V. III-132.

[187] *Id.* at III-133.

[188] *Id.* at III-134.

[189] *Id.* at III-139.

[190] *State v. Kirstin Blaise Lobato*, Case Number C177394, Transcript, October 2, 2006, XVI. 62.

[191] *Id.* at 63-65.

[192] *Id.* at 66.

[193] *Id.* at 75.

[194] *Id.* at 75-82.

[195] *Id.* at 80-81.

[196] *Id.* at 81.

[197] *Id.* at 82. Although Greenberger didn't mention it, Vega's prosecution bias may have been a reflection of her former employment in the Clark County District Attorney's Office, where she worked with Kephart.

[198] *Id.* at 83.

[199] *State v. Kirstin Blaise Lobato*, Case Number C177394, Transcript, October 4, 2006, XVIII. 8.

[200] *Id.* at 10.

[201] *Id.* at 11.

[202] *Id.* at 12. Ashley Lobato was also never interviewed by any officer with the LVMPD, see, *State v. Kirstin Blaise Lobato*, Case Number C177394, Transcript, October 3, 2006, XVII, 136:

Q. Have the police ever contacted you with respect to your sister's situation?

A. No.

[203] Q.— you using methamphetamine? When were you using methamphetamine?

A. When was I using it?

Q. Mm-hmm.

A. Between 1998 and 2002. *State v. Kirstin Blaise Lobato*, Case Number C177394, Transcript, October 4, 2006, XVIII. 19.

[204] *Id.* at 67.

[205] *Id.* at 18.

[206] *State v. Kirstin Blaise Lobato*, Case Number C177394, Transcript, October 4, 2006, XVII. 188-189:

Q. What time did you get home from work that evening?

A. It could've been between midnight and 1 o'clock in the morning, somewhere in that area.

Q. Was that the standard time you would get home?

A. Yes.

[207] *Id.* at 190-191.

[208] *State v. Kirstin Blaise Lobato*, Case Number C177394, Transcript, September 18, 2006, VI. 62. (Austria direct.)

[209] *Id.* at 119. (Brown direct.)

[210] *Id.* at 63-65. (Austria direct.)

[211] *Id.* at 82-84. (Austria cross-examination.)

[212] It is notable that the Lobato family moved to Ontario, California after Blaise's 2002 conviction, and so it can't credibly be suggested that some of those alibi witnesses, including those who have also moved from Lincoln County, tailored their testimony to aid Blaise. Some of the alibi witnesses weren't even friends of hers, but merely acquaintances.

[213] The McCrosky's were gone over the 4th of July, 2001, so they testified that from about July 6 until July 20, when the police took Blaise's car, they had not seen it moved and it was continuously parked in the same place on the street behind a utility trailer in front of the Lobato's house. Mr. McCrosky takes a walk every morning, and he testified Blaise's car was in the same place every morning.

[214] Q. Now with regard to the purpose of DNA, it's to look for DNA to help, make conclusions, I believe is what you said, your testing?

A. Yes.

Q. Okay. Now the fact that you find a person's DNA on an item you tested, that doesn't tell you whether or not they did the crime, correct?

A. Absolutely not.

Q. It only tells you whether or not their biological matter is on the piece of evidence you tested?

A. Correct.

Q. So the conclusions you draw are just whether or not somebody touched something or drank from something, not whether or not they've committed a crime?

A. Absolutely.

State v. Kirstin Blaise Lobato, Case Number C177394, Transcript, October 2, 2006, XVI-47 (Cross examination.)

[215] The July 7, 2001 tests were conducted by Associated Pathologists Laboratories, 4230 Burnham Ave., Las Vegas. The test detected marijuana in her system, but no other drug. Interestingly, Bailey's blood test found only cocaine and alcohol (.011) in his system – but no marijuana.

[216] Michelle Austria and Paul "Rusty" Brown both testified to seeing Blaise on Saturday (and Sunday), and they both saw her car parked in front of her parent's house. Brown testified on cross-examination by Greenberger:

Q. Do you recall seeing Blaise the weekend after the 4th of July, the 7th and the 8th, in Panaca?

A. Yes.

Q. Do you recall seeing her red Fiero still parked in front of her house during that time period?

A. Yes

State v. Kirstin Blaise Lobato, Case Number C177394, Transcript, September 18, 2006, VI. 127.

[217] Brown testified he saw Blaise and her car on the 8th, but he wasn't asked a specific time. His girlfriend went four-wheeling with Blaise at 11:30 a.m., so it is a safe presumption that he saw her about that time or after they returned in the early afternoon around 1 p.m. *Id.* at 127

[218] Becky Lobato testified that Chris Carrington was present when she made a telephone to her sister at 6:43 p.m.:

By Mr. Schieck:

Q. When you made the call to your sister in Ft, Collins, Colorado at 6:43 p.m. on July 8th, lasting 12 minutes, who else was present when you made that call?

A. My niece, Blaise, Chris, We were in the garage when I made the call.

State v. Kirstin Blaise Lobato, Case Number C177394, Transcript, October 4, 2006, XVIII. 106. (Direct examination)

[219] Chris Carrington is the one possible exception, except that the prosecution's challenge to his testimony about seeing Blaise each day from Friday July 6 through Sunday July 8 is mitigated by the fact that his testimony was consistent with the testimony of many other witnesses whose recollections of seeing Blaise in Panaca from July 2 to July 9 were not seriously challenged, and in some cases conceded by the prosecution.

[220] *State v. Kirstin Blaise Lobato*, Case Number C177394, Transcript, October 4, 2006, XVIII. 67.

[221] Statement to LVMPD, *supra,* at 3-4.

[222] DiGiacomo made variations of this argument five separate times to the jury, and Kephart did so once in an extended argument that went on for three paragraphs in the transcript.

[223] The PowerPoint presentation listed as a "fact" that Blaise was in Las Vegas on July 6, when all the trial evidence – including that testified to by prosecution witnesses – was that she was in Panaca from the afternoon of July 2 until the early morning of July 9.

[224] All quotes from Schieck's closing argument, October 5, 2006. *The State of Nevada vs. Kirstin Blaise Lobato*, Case No. C177394 (Eighth Judicial District Court, Clark County, Nevada), Trial Transcript, Vol. XIX, October 5, 2006, Defendant's Closing Argument, XIX 150-185.

[225] Kephart made an extended argument about this that went on for three paragraphs in the transcript DiGiacomo made variations of this argument five separate times during her opening argument to the jury.

[226] See the following three articles: Joshua Longobardy, "Kirsten Blaise Lobato is accused in a gruesome slaying. Did she do it?," *Las Vegas Weekly*, October 12-18, 2006. ("Both the prosecution and the defense thought the jurors, tired, irritable and deadlocked, came to a middle ground with their verdict."); and, Matt Pordum, "Woman convicted of killing homeless man in 'compromise' verdict," *Court TV* website, October 6, 2006. ("Both the prosecution and defense agreed that the jury's decision was a "compromise." Special Public Defender David Schieck ... theorized that the jury was deadlocked, but tired, after the four-week trial. "This jury was done with the case," Schieck said. "There were probably strong opinions on both guilt and innocence in this case and no one would give in so they agreed to pick something in the middle." ... "Prosecutor Bill "Kephart said he wasn't happy about the jury's verdict, but he "understood their compromise.""); and also, "Woman convicted in slaying retrial," K.C. Howard, Las Vegas *Review-Journal*, October 7, 2006. ("In the end, they reached a middle ground." Defense attorney David Schieck)

[227] Tienken's Statement, *supra* at 5 and 11.

[228] *State v. Kirstin Blaise Lobato*, Case Number C177394, Transcript, September 18, 2006, VI. 65. (Austria direct.)

[229] *State v. Kirstin Blaise Lobato*, Case Number C177394, Transcript, September 20, 2006, VIII. 21-26. (Simms' cross-examination.)
[230] *Id.* at 79.

[231] Also, Dixie Tienken said in her statement that Blaise told her that she was assaulted when it was "dark."

[232] On July 8, 2001, nautical dawn, which was at 4:24 a.m., is when there is enough light for objects to be distinguishable and outdoor activities can be engaged in without artificial light. Civil dawn, which was at 5:01 a.m., is when there is enough light for a person to legally operate their vehicle without their headlights on. Sunrise, which was at 5:30 a.m., is when the is sun physically visible above the horizon and there is direct sunlight. For the times of dawn and sunrise, see, http://www.weatherunderground.com (last visited November 2, 2007). For the definitions of nautical and civil dawn, and sunrise, see Astronomical Terms on the National Oceanic and Atmospheric Administration website at, http://www.srh.noaa.gov/ffc/html/gloss3.shtml (last visited Nov. 2, 2007).

[233] This actually grants the prosecution a concession that technically is not correct. According to NOAA, "astronomical dawn" is the time at which "the sun starts lightening the sky. Prior to this time, the sky is completely dark." Astronomical dawn on July 8 was at 3:43 a.m., which was seven minutes *prior* to Simms' most remote estimated time of Bailey's death. However, since it wasn't until nautical dawn, which was at 4:24 a.m, that there was enough light to distinguish objects and engage in activities without artificial light, that is time that will be used as when "dawn" was on July 8, so that there can be no quibbling about what the earliest time was that it would no longer be "night" and "dark" as Blaise described it as being when she was attacked, and which Tienken said was told by Blaise during their conversation in early July 2001. For details about the source of the definitions and times of dawn and sunrise on July 8, see the preceding endnote.

[234] Distance reported by mapquest.com, http://mapquest.com (last visited October 24, 2007)

[235] *State v. Kirstin Blaise Lobato*, Case Number C177394, Transcript, September 29, 2006, XV. 47.

[236] Q. How long did that trip take on the way back from Panaca?
A. About two and a half hours probably.
State v. Kirstin Blaise Lobato, Case Number C177394, Transcript, September 27, 2006, XIII. 95. Cross-examination of Thowsen by Schieck.

[237] (72 mph x 3 hrs)/2.5 hours = 86.4 mph
[238] (72 mph x3 hrs)/2 hours = 108 mph
[239] *State v. Kirstin Blaise Lobato*, Case Number C177394, Transcript, October 4, 2006, XVIII. 136-137. (Cross-examination of Becky Lobato by DiGiacomo.)

[240] Mapquest.com's estimated driving time of 2 hours 47 minutes for the 171 mile trip from Panaca to Las Vegas. Source, http://mapquest.com (last visited October 24, 2007)

[241] The 30 minute estimate of time spent in Las Vegas is deliberately unrealistic to illustrate the implausibility of the prosecution's claimed scenario of the crime. Blaise said she drove to her friend Jeremy Davis' house after being attacked to clean herself up. Davis lived on the Las Vegas' eastside at 4827 Meredith Ave. While this is about 1 mile from the Budget Suites Hotel, according to mapquest.com it is 8 miles and 15 minutes driving time from where Bailey was murdered on Vegas' westside. So that would only allow her 15 minutes to kill Bailey, shower, and do whatever else she would have done in Las Vegas and on her way to and from there from Panaca.

[242] *State v. Kirstin Blaise Lobato*, Case Number C177394, Transcript, October 4, 2006, XVIII. 101-2.

[243] Kephart specifically inferred the three were lying during his rebuttal argument. *State v. Kirstin Blaise Lobato*, Case Number C177394, Transcript, October 5, 2006, XIX. 189-190.

[244] Blaise positively asserted in her July 20, 2001 statement that she was assaulted at night. According to weather records, dawn was at 4:24 a.m. on July 8, 2001, so if her assault would occurred on that date it would have happened prior to then. Source: History for Las Vegas, Nevada, July 8, 2001, http://weatherunderground.com (last visited November 2, 2007).

[245] "The State wants you to go back to the 24 hour time frame, which is not – which is to a greater probability. But as the doctor described, it's a bell curve. This is the bigger probability, As you get out toward the edges it flattens out. I'm sure you're all familiar with bell curves.

I tried to draw one, sort of like that, a bell curve, And the greater probability is the major portion of it. And if she – if you believe she was there during that period of time which the death occurred to a reasonable medical certainty, you must acquit.

Now I thought it would be great if I tried to put all the other testimony in that related to the alibi in order to cover the reasonable medical certainty time, as you can see, it's a little bit difficult to do. I'm gonna try to do that by arguing with you." *State v. Kirstin Blaise Lobato*, Case Number C177394, Transcript, October 5, 2006, XIX. 174. (Schieck closing.)

[246] John Tabak, *Probability and Statistics: The Science of Uncertainty*, (New York: Facts on File (May 2004)), pp. 37-44, esp. 41-43. Among other things Abraham de Moivre studied mortality statistics and he laid the foundation of the theory of annuities. Moivre also has the distinction of accurately predicting the day of his own death in 1754.

[247] *Id*. at 42.

[248] *Id*. at xiv.

[249] *Id*. at 41.

[250] The bell curve probabilities are based on the calculations performed by Amy Ehrlich, a Mathematics Instructor at Highline Community College in Des Moines, Washington. They were emailed to Hans Sherrer on December 3, 2007. However, Hans Sherrer takes responsibility for all the bell curve analysis in this manuscript, and any interpretation of Ms. Ehrlich's calculations. Her calculations were based a mean of 12:50 p.m., a standard deviation of 91.84 minutes, and a 95% probability that the time of death was between 9:50 a.m. and 3:50 p.m. A TI-84 plus Silver Edition was used to make the calculations.

[251] This is for the year 2004. The odds are, see, "The Odds of Dying From ...., The National Safety Council website, http://www.nsc.org/lrs/statinfo/odds.htm (last visited November 12, 2007)

[252] The probability that Bailey died at 12:50 p.m. is 50%. 62,623,812*50% = 31,311,906.

[253] Also suggesting a time of death closer to the discovery of Bailey's body is Simms' admission that the covering of his body both retarded the loss of his body heat and concentrated the ambient outside air temperature under the covering, which would have accelerated the rigor mortis process of what it would have naturally been if his body had been exposed – thus possibly making it appear he died longer from the time his body was examined than he actually did. *State v. Kirstin Blaise Lobato*, Case Number C177394, Transcript, September 19, 2006, VII. 147-149 (Direct testimony) VII.; *State v. Kirstin Blaise Lobato*, Case Number C177394, Transcript, September 20, 2006, VIII. 18-25 (Cross-examination)

[254] Nautical twilight was at 4:24 a.m., which is when night begins to end. Civil twilight was at 5:01 a.m. which is when there was enough light that a person could legally turn their headlights off. Sunrise was at 5:30 a.m. See, http://www.weatherunderground.com (last visited November 2, 2007).

[255] Civil twilight was at 5:01 a.m. See, http://www.weatherunderground.com (last visited November 2, 2007).

[256] The average high temperature in July is 104 °F and the average low temperature is 78 °F, with an average mean temperature of 91 °F. On July 8, 2001 the high temperature was 95 °F and the mean temperature was 84 °F. Source: History for Las Vegas, Nevada, July 8, 2001, http://weatherunderground.com (last visited August 1, 2007).

[257] *State v. Kirstin Blaise Lobato*, Case Number C177394, Transcript, September 19, 2006, VII. 147. ("Q. Okay. What type of things would effect rigor mortis. A. [by Simms] One of the most important things is the ambient temperature outside." (Direct testimony)

[258] *Id*. at 147. ("A. ... If you have a very, very warm environment, it can go through those phases very, very rapidly.") (Direct testimony)

[259] *State v. Kirstin Blaise Lobato*, Case Number C177394, Transcript, September 20, 2006, VIII. 19-20. (Cross-examination)

[260] *Id*. at 24. (cross-examination)

[261] *Id*. at 19. (Cross-examination); *State v. Kirstin Blaise Lobato*, Case Number C177394, Transcript, September 19, 2006, VII. 147-149. (Direct testimony).

[262] William Henry Howell, *A Text-book of Physiology for Medical Students and Physicians* (Philadelphia: William B. Saunders & Co, 1906), 49. ("Death after great muscular exertion, as in the case of hunted animals, or soldiers killed in battle, is usually followed quickly by muscle rigor, indeed, in extreme cases it may develop almost immediately.") *Id*.

See also, Keith Herber, *The Keeper's Companion: A Core Book for Keepers* (Chaosium, Inc. 2000), 136. ("If a person had an elevated body temperature, either through physical exertion or fever, or if a person had died in a hot environment, rigor mortis and decomposition will progress much more rapidly than it will in persons with lower body or environmental temperatures.") *Id*.

[263] *State v. Kirstin Blaise Lobato*, Case Number C177394, Transcript, September 20, 2006, VIII. 23. (Cross-examination)

[264] *State v. Lobato*, Case No. C177394, Reporter's Transcript of Preliminary Hearing, August 7, 2001, 32-33. (emphasis added to original)

[265] Q. Do you have opinion when this person died?

A. No. And I think the subject was brought up that wasn't an issue at the time of the case. I may be able to do some testing and come up with a broad window, if that's an issue that will serve the court. I don't have any opinion as of right now.

Q. Could it have been 48 hours?

A. No, sir.

Q. What window are we talking about?

A. The body wasn't manifesting any significant degree of decomposition, so I would say he had died a lot closer to the time he was discovered than not. So it was definitely within 24 hours. And probably more likely than not some time within 12 hours of when he was discovered.

Q. You indicated there's some tests you could have done with the fluid in the eyes; is that correct?

A. That is correct.

Q. Is that test still available to us?

A. Yes, sir.

State v. Lobato, Case No. C177394, Reporter's Transcript of Preliminary Hearing, August 7, 2001, 32-33. (emphasis added to original)

[266] Statement to Las Vegas Metropolitan Police Department by Richard Shott, Event #010708-2410, 1:23 a.m., July 9, 2001.

[267] Considering the critical importance of Bailey's time of death to excluding any possibility that Blaise could have been involved in his murder, it is somewhat astonishing that her lawyers for her first trial did not make any effort to follow through on having the "potassium eye fluid test" conducted after ME Simms testified at her preliminary hearing that the test could be performed. Nor did her lawyers for her second trial make any effort to have the test performed. If Bailey's body was buried, his eyeball(s) may still be extant. If so, then one or both may be able to be tested by the "potassium eye fluid test" to narrow his possible time of death to the evening of July 8 when it is known to 100% certainty that Blaise was in Panaca. See the discussion about this test in Chapter 1: Medical Examiner Simms estimates Bailey's time of death.

[268] Benjamin Franklin, "Letter to Benjamin Vaughn, March 14, 1785." Quoted in *The Quotable Founding Fathers: A Treasury of 2,500 Wise and Witty Quotations from the Men and Women Who Created America*, ed. Buckner F. Melton (Potomac Books 2005).

[269] Sir John Fortescue, *De Laudibus Legum Angliae*, c. 1470.

[270] Sir William Blackstone, *Commentaries on the Laws of England*, 1765-69.

[271] Increase Mather, *Cases of Conscience Concerning Evil Spirits Personating Men*, October 3, 1692. (Boston: Benjamin Harris at the London Coffee-House, 1693.)

[272] Moses Maimonides, *The Commandments, Neg. Comm.* 290, at 269-271 (Charles B. Chavel trans., 1967). Maimonides argued that executing a defendant on anything less than absolute certainty would lead to a slippery slope of decreasing burdens of proof, until we would be convicting merely "according to the judge's caprice." *Id.* at 269-271. Maimonides' concern was maintaining respect for law, and he saw errors of commission much more threatening than errors of omission.

[273] Also, Dixie Tienken said in her statement that Blaise told her that she was assaulted when it was "dark."

[274] Based on Simms' estimate of Bailey's "possible" time of death, there is a .13% probability that he died between 3:50 a.m. and 5:50 a.m. Consequently there would be less than a .037% probability (.13/(120/34)) for the 34 minute period from 4:24 a.m. to 3:50 a.m.

[275] Blaise said in her statement that after getting away from her assailant that she got in her car and drove away.

[276] The only three points of incidental coincidence was her assault was by a black man (much taller and heavier than Bailey), a sharp object of some sort was involved in both incidents (her knife had a much shorter blade (3-1/2 to 4") than the scissors or knife used to stab Bailey that had upwards of a 6" edge), and both events occurred in Las Vegas (but eight miles apart in different areas of the city). (See Table 1, p. 17) Those are minor details because the use of a sharp object to fend off or commit a crime involving a black man as the perpetrator or the victim is common in Las Vegas.

[277] 3:50 a.m. to 7:50 p.m. is 16 hours, and the 34 minutes of pre-dawn darkness from 3:50 to 4:24 a.m. is 3.5% of that span of time.

[278] Based on Simms' estimate of Bailey's "possible" time of death, there is less than a .037% probability that he died during 34 minute period from the beginning of dawn at 4:24 a.m. to 3:50 a.m.

[279] Peter O'Connell, "Murder Charge: Cut Result of Attack, Teen Says," Las Vegas *Review-Journal*, July 25, 2001.

[280] "It has long been black letter law in Nevada that the *corpus delicti* of a crime must be proven independently of the defendant's extra-judicial admissions." *Edwards v. State*, 132 P.3d 581 (Nev. 04/27/2006).

[281] For a discussion of the dominance of bureaucratic processes in the United States and how they contribute to injustice, see, Hans Sherrer, "The Inhumanity of Government Bureaucracies," *The Independent Review*, Vol. 5, No. 2 (Fall 2000): 249-264.

www.ingramcontent.com/pod-product-compliance
Lightning Source LLC
Chambersburg PA
CBHW081138170526
45165CB00008B/2718